D0939150

Reinventing Myself: Memoirs of a Retired Professor

By Marlys Marshall Styne

Copyright © 2006 by Marlys Marshall Styne

ISBN 0-7414-3208-0

Published by:

1094 *New DeHaven Street, Suite 100*
West Conshohocken, PA 19428-2713
Info@buybooksontheweb.com
www.buybooksontheweb.com
Toll-free (877) BUY BOOK
Local Phone (610) 941-9999
Fax (610) 941-9959

Printed in the United States of America

Printed on Recycled Paper

Published May 2006

Table of Contents

With Thanks:

To Jack Helbig and Jill Pollack of StoryStudio Chicago and my friend Margot Adler Wallace for encouraging me to write.

To my friend Pat Hawley for being a willing and extraordinary proofreader. She is not responsible for any errors that might remain.

To my brother, John Marshall, for his insightful comments and his computer advice.

To Jane Wagoner for being a supportive colleague and friend for many years.

To all the inventors and developers of computers and software who have made writing, revising, and communicating so easy.

Preface

Retired seven years, widowed six years, childless, seventy-three years old, depressed: I decided to reinvent my life through writing. This required looking at who I was, who I am, and who I want to be. Yet this book is not just about me; it's also about the experiences that have affected me and the people—and the cats—with whom I have shared them.

As memories do not appear in a logical, chronological order, neither do the essays in this book. Some date back to the 1980's and 1990's, including those written during my long teaching career. Some deal with what's happened in the recent past. Others look forward toward events that have not happened yet. In the course of a long life, memories overlap; one experience may lead to both thoughts about an earlier experience and speculation about a future one.

These memoirs represent how I see—or saw—many of the people and events in my life. Should anyone feel insulted or unfairly described, I apologize.

In Gratitude

This book was inspired, in part, by my mother's 1997 autobiography, *My First Eighty-Six Years: a Midwestern Life*. My mother, Violet Marshall Funston, is now ninety-four, and she lives in a nursing home in Northfield, Minnesota. She is wheelchair bound; her physical health is poor, and her life has become difficult. However, as she wrote in her autobiography, she is still trying to "maintain [her] positive outlook on life and help others see the brighter side." I thank her for putting the story of her life into print, and I thank her for passing along her father's message that she could do anything she wanted to do and should never be afraid to follow her dreams. My dreams may be somewhat different from hers, but I shall continue trying to follow them.

I. Family and Aging

Wedding Reception, 6/27/70

Marlys and Jules, Thanksgiving 1999

2

Autobiography of a Professor, 1995

I was born Marlys May Marshall on October 12, 1932, in Whitewater, Wisconsin, and grew up on a dairy farm. My ancestry was English, French, and German. My father, Clifford William Marshall, was a Business Administration graduate of St. Olaf College, Northfield, Minnesota, and my mother, Violet Uhl Marshall, had completed two years as an English major at Whitewater State Teachers College, now the University of Wisconsin at Whitewater, before her marriage. Having unusually well-educated parents for that time and place, I grew up believing that it was my destiny to go to college. My brother, John Clifford Marshall, Ph.D., who is now a chemistry professor and computer expert at St. Olaf College, discovered the benefits of education later.

I graduated as valedictorian of the Class of 1950, Whitewater College High School, a school that no longer exists, having participated in every literary, musical, and student government activity offered. I ignored only sports activities. My mother had taken a job as manager of the local Sears Order Office to bolster the family finances, so I was able to attend Luther College, Decorah, Iowa, in the fall of 1950 with a dream of playing clarinet in the Luther College Concert Band. I played in the band, as last chair or next-to-last, for two years, but discovered that my major interests and talents were in literature and writing, not in music. I eventually played in the less prestigious marching band and sang in the women's chorus. I soon joined the college newspaper staff as probably the shyest reporter ever; I still remember the agony of having to interview a minor opera singer who was appearing on a community concert program. Somehow I succeeded without fainting from fear and got a byline in the paper, and my newspaper career was launched. I eventually became executive editor of *College Chips*, and even a college columnist for the local newspaper.

My first mentor at Luther College was English Professor David T. Nelson (now deceased), who not only gave me all A's, but hired me to mark mechanical errors on his other students' papers. Thus I got my first paper-grading experience at the tender age of eighteen! A later mentor was Literature Professor John Bale, now retired, who came to Luther during my senior year and whom I met and talked with this past September at the ALSC conference in Minneapolis. I also remember Professor Weston Noble, then the choir and band director and still the choir director. He knew me not for my mediocre musical talents, but as a roommate of music majors and as a newspaper correspondent reporting on band tours. He taught me that music and writing are both serious activities requiring extensive practice. I was surprised when he recognized me on the occasion of the thirtieth reunion of my class.

After graduating Magna cum Laude in 1954 with a degree in English, I was broke, without teaching credentials, and jobless. I knew I wanted to go to graduate school, but I couldn't afford it. I moved to Minneapolis and got a secretarial job at the University of Minnesota Law Library; I also started taking one graduate course at a time. My most memorable professors at Minnesota were Leo Marx (American Literature) and Samuel Holt Monk (nineteenth-century British Literature), the latter, now deceased, one of the editors of the famous *Norton Anthology of English Literature* that I use in my classes today. I eventually became a full-time student, finished my course work, and went to Morgantown, West Virginia, to teach at West Virginia University; my master's degree was awarded in 1957. At West Virginia I felt young, inexperienced, and naïve. My "real education" came from my students and from my more sophisticated teaching colleagues from Chicago and New York. I felt like a sort of second-class citizen when male colleagues of equal or lesser education and experience got chances to teach literature while my female colleagues and I did not.

The highlight of my two years of teaching at West Virginia was the trip I took to Europe with the Experiment in International Living during the summer of 1957. I stayed with a family in Edinburgh, Scotland, and then fulfilled my wildest dreams of the time, to see Anne Hathaway's Cottage, Westminster Abbey, and the Eiffel Tower. I also bicycled in the highlands of Scotland. My passion for travel continues to this day.

I left West Virginia for a teaching assistantship at the University of Wisconsin, Madison, for 1958-59. I was on my way, I thought, to my Ph.D. in English, but that was not to be. I left at the end of the first semester to marry Robert Carter Clark, the son of one of my favorite American Literature professors, the late Harry Hayden Clark. We moved to Glenview, a Chicago suburb, and my career at Wright College was soon to begin.

After a short career as a secretary in Northbrook, I walked into the old Wright College on Austin Avenue and was hired almost immediately as an evening teacher by Sumner Scott, Chair of the English Department, and his able secretary, Elsie Temple. That was the fall semester, 1959, and the rest, as they say, is history. I have never left Wright except for a one-year sabbatical in 1984-85, during which I "discovered" computers and made them a big part of my academic life. I've always taught English 101, with occasional forays into English 100 and 102. I also teach fiction and the traditional surveys of English and American Literature. I take pride in promoting Wright's recent expansion of its literature offerings.

At Wright, I've also taken great pride in the awards I've received, up to and including this year's Distinguished Service Professor 1995-96 honor. I won the Faculty Council-sponsored Distinguished Service Award for 1991-92, as well as the Phi Theta Kappa Outstanding Teacher Award for 1994-95.

The non-academic highlight of my life was my marriage in 1970 to my second husband, Julian H. (Jules) Styne. Through him I gained two grown step-children to make up for the children I was never able to have, and later, three step grandchildren. Jules has patiently overlooked my lack of housewifely skills and my workaholic devotion to my job, and has provided emotional support I couldn't have lived without. He retired in 1992 after more than twenty years as a Deputy U.S. Marshal, but still works in the local Marshal's office periodically. I was proud to speak at Jules' retirement party.

Through Jules, I learned to love motorcycle touring, despite the unfortunate Austrian accident in 1976 that caused my knee problems. We have toured the Alps of Germany, Austria, Switzerland, France, and northern Italy four times and Russia once on a motorcycle, in addition to many trips within the United States and Canada. We have also traveled extensively by more conventional means, with trips to England, Greece, and Spain the most recent. On December 30, 1995, we're off to Rome, Florence, and Venice.

I am happy to be a five-year breast cancer survivor, and also the oldest woman still touring occasionally with our local motorcycle club, the Streeterville Scramblers. I appreciate all the help given me by my mother, Violet Funston of Northfield, Minnesota, and Scottsdale, Arizona. She completed college after I received my master's degree, and she enjoyed a career as an elementary school English teacher and librarian in northern Wisconsin before her retirement. She is still alive and well at eighty-four, and still serves as my inspiration.

My plans for the future include more of what I've been doing: hard work and frequent travel, health permitting. Eventually, I shall retire.

Aging in November, 2002

November 1, 2002, is a Friday, a day of TGIF euphoria and making weekend plans for many, but not for me. I am seventy years old and retired from my forty-year-plus job as a community college professor. As usual, Friday just brings reminders of the boring weekend ahead. Weekends are only occasionally enlivened by a party or a play or a solo trip to the movies, but none are scheduled this weekend. It's not that I don't have friends, but most are younger, far away, occupied with their families, and/or still working in demanding jobs. Mainly a hard-working loner in my younger days, I just don't have a large number of close friends to depend on. I can't blame anyone but myself for that. I don't have a family nearby, either.

Even though daylight saving time has ended, it is still dark at 4:00 a.m., my usual rising time. Why so early? Somehow, falling asleep in the recliner at 9:00 p.m., going to bed, and waking up at 4:00 have become habits–very useful ones when I regularly taught early English classes to sleepy community college students. But now? With hours like mine, it is nearly impossible to stay awake for an evening opera performance or a party, or even a restaurant dinner begun at a fashionable hour. No wonder senior citizens attend matinees and swarm to the restaurants' early bird specials.

Aging. It happens to most people, but I still feel young most of the time. Where have the gray hair and the fat come from? Every spring I am ready for a new beginning, represented by the bright red, pink, and purple petunias on my balcony. Now, the few remaining flowers, surprisingly long-lasting this year, are pale and drooping, waiting for the oft-predicted first hard frost. The few trees I can see from my balcony bear yellow leaves and a few bare branches. On windy days, I can see the leaves drifting toward the ground, or at least to the roofs of the surrounding mid-rise condo buildings and stores. A few blocks away, the high rises of downtown Chicago tower in the background, far above any trees that survive in that area.

As I frequently pointed out to my literature students, poets often use the passing seasons to symbolize human life cycles: spring for birth and rebirth, summer for maturity and fulfillment, autumn for decline, winter for death and sleep. Now bits and pieces of poetry sometimes invade my mind as proof that I was right when I tried to convince my students of the relevance of poetry and the connections between literature and life. Today it is Shakespeare's "Sonnet 73": "That time of year thou mayst in me behold / When yellow leaves, or none, or few, do hang / Upon those boughs which shake against the cold, / Bare ruin'd choirs, where late the sweet birds sang."

November first. It begins as a cold but sunny day, with a hazy blue sky. The sounds of garbage trucks in the alley and a child's footsteps in the condo above are there as usual, but I hardly notice such things any more. All in all, mine is a quiet and very comfortable condo, and I am glad to live here. "Traditional/eclectic," my interior designer called the decor, perhaps in jest. Of course the place features beautiful oak floors, granite counter tops, stainless steel appliances, and a marble fireplace, the trendy upgrades of the moment.

The living room features a dark green leather sofa and recliner, dark green brocade drapes, an oriental rug, a gigantic entertainment center, and miscellaneous small pieces of furniture from my old house, including a pair of china lamps that were a gift in the early 1960's and were considered antiques even then. There are also some "fake antiques," the kind with little flaws purposely created by the manufacturers. How did they create that wavy, old-looking glass in the china cabinet? Did someone really hit the lamp table with chains to create those marks? Why?

The walls are adorned with framed works of art, most of it purchased at art fairs over the years and most of it featuring cats. Yes, I am a cat person, and my aging Persian cat, Lyon, is my roommate and companion. Then, there is a 1970's Phil Rowe metal wall sculpture, a collection of green metal flowers and bugs climbing the dining room's west wall. This hung over the spiral staircase at the house on Cleveland Avenue, and it has been rehung exactly as originally installed, minus the Chicago artist's signature. Near the sculpture wall is the kitchen with its stainless steel, granite, and oak. The kitchen is lovely, but it's a room where I spend very little time.

Lyon has his own room, a small bathroom with a colorful shower curtain and towels and etchings of Anne Hathaway's Cottage and the Houses of Parliament on the walls. I wish that Lyon were neater, since he has a habit of spilling bits of both his food and his kitty litter onto the tile floor. This is the room least likely to be neat and clean.

Across a small hallway from that bathroom is my study, complete with books, a computer, a color laser printer, a comfortable office chair, lamps, storage cabinets, and a small "sleep sofa" for an occasional guest. As of November 1, the sofa has been used only once, by my visiting brother.

Above the sofa hang the usual memorabilia of a teacher's life: college diplomas, awards, the be-ribboned NISOD (National Institute of Staff and Organizational Development) medal I always remove from its frame to wear with my blue robe to college graduation ceremonies, even a photo showing me receiving a service award from Mayor Richard M. Daley. That man gets around! I know of at least three other residents of this small building who have pictures of themselves with Daley. Politics is a strange business in Chicago; I consider myself apolitical.

To the left of the awards wall hangs a plaque containing three silver coins on a red background: two 1970 Kennedy half-dollars, displayed back and front, and a larger coin that reads, "25th Anniversary, 1995." Yes, Jules and I married in 1970, and our silver anniversary was an important milestone. As it turned out, we didn't quite make it to our 30th anniversary, but we were close when Jules died in March 2000. I remember that the 25th anniversary party invitation included the words, "And they said it would never last!" Well, it did, and it was a happy marriage!

Books, books, books: anthologies of English and American literature, dictionaries, computer software manuals, and many others. The bookshelves above the computer desk also feature a color photo of me at my desk in my English Department chairperson's office at the college. That was my "home away from home" for the last seven years of my teaching career. The photo was taken in 1999, my retirement year. That wasn't so long ago. I wonder why I looked so much better then?

Just to the right of the computer desk hang two pictures. One shows a charming street scene from Bergen, Norway. The Scandinavian coastal cruise was the last one I took with Jules, in 1999. The scenery was beautiful, with the North Cape and the midnight sun at what seemed like the top of the world. However, Jules got sick on the ship on the way down the coast. Was it the food, or a warning that his good health had come to an end?

Beneath the Bergen picture (Bergen was the final stop before the trip ended) is a color photo of a red-and-white house with a large garage. This is the house we purchased back in 1968 and worked on for thirty years. With the endless additions, remodeling, painting, and repairs, the house was a long-term project. Now it belongs to someone else. I loved living there, but as my thoughts drift back to the condo, I am glad to be rid of the responsibility of an aging house.

There are still some reminders of the house here in the condo. Past the large walk-in closet, in the master bedroom, a large room with a skyline view to the east, sits one of the few pieces of furniture moved from the house, and much earlier, from the old Wisconsin farmhouse where I grew up. It is a Victorian secretary desk with a cloudy mirror and a pull-down top, a bit battered but looking much as it has always looked. I remember that this was in the farmhouse during my childhood, and probably belonged to my paternal grandparents once. On the whole, it is an ugly piece of furniture, but I wouldn't part with it. A red-and-white stained glass Tiffany-style chandelier from the bedroom of our red-and-white house on Cleveland Avenue hangs from the ceiling nearby.

The queen-size bed features a Tempur-Pedic mattress on an adjustable bed frame, just the thing for an aging woman. The carpet in the bedroom, as in the study and hallway, is beige. Muted plaid draperies and a red-flowered bedspread with matching ruffled pillows give the room color. Like the living room and study, the bedroom features a door to the small balcony where the petunias are taking their final bows for the season.

Finally, the master bath is a wonder: beige marble floor, two sinks, a huge bathtub, and a marble shower stall with a bench. One person doesn't need two sinks, but I appreciate the spaciousness and luxury of the room. The two small rugs are pseudo-oriental, and the towels are red.

After my mental tour of the condo, I come back to the reality of sitting in my green leather recliner with Lyon and a crossword puzzle book in my lap vying for attention. Lyon is the ultimate lap cat, almost used to having a book balanced on his back. Yes, since retirement, I have become quite a puzzle aficionado. I read somewhere that doing puzzles keeps the mind sharp. I hope so. I haven't had much success with *New York Times* crosswords, but those in the *Chicago Tribune* seem manageable.

November: there is something about the beginning of this month that invites retrospection. I begin to remember people and events from my earlier life: my wonderful husband Jules, motorcycle enthusiast and Deputy U.S. Marshal, who died in 2000 of pancreatic cancer after a short but horrible illness; my first husband, Bob, whose only fault was being boring at a time when I was searching for excitement. It was a short marriage that just didn't work out. I wonder about friends and colleagues I've lost track of over the years.

I remember my travels, usually with Jules, often by motorcycle but also on planes, trains, buses, automobiles, and cruise ships. From England in 1957 to China in 2001, I have been to so many places that I often have a "been there, done that" feeling. Jules and I traveled in Germany, Austria, Switzerland, Italy, Scotland, France, Spain, Portugal, Morocco, Greece, Turkey, Australia, New Zealand, Mexico, Costa Rica, Denmark, Sweden, and Russia. Can I travel more? The trip to China and Thailand without Jules in 2001 was fine, but a bit lonely.

Beside the recliner is a collection of travel brochures. I am considering a Danube River cruise, Eastern Europe to the Black Sea, next June. In the old days, I would have said, "Let's go." Now it is time to think about the problems of being older and alone. Can I handle all the walking during tours away from the boat? Can I get–and afford–a single cabin? Do I need to fly business class to avoid circulation problems in my legs? What will I do about Lyon? I've had a cat sitter during previous trips, but now Lyon needs two insulin shots a day. No regular cat sitter will take the job, even if she were able to coax Lyon out of one of his favorite hiding places. It might have to be the vet hospital, where Lyon staged a hunger strike on his last visit.

My condo tour and travel reveries over for the moment, I return to my crossword puzzle and my cat. It is time to read the morning *Tribune*. Still, it is tempting to go on remembering the past at this time when I feel that "In me thou seest the glowing of such fire / That on the ashes of [her] youth doth lie."

Somehow, on this November day, I need to deal with the problems of aging.

On Growing Old, 2006

Occasionally, after I've uttered a self-deprecatory statement about aging, someone will say, "You're not old!" I've noticed that I don't hear that as often as I used to, though. The wrinkles, the gray hair, sometimes artfully disguised by highlights but always there, and my trouble rising from a seated position are dead giveaways. Senior discounts come automatically now. I'm over seventy, and it shows.

When you're young, "old" means over thirty, and then forty, and then fifty, then sixty, and then—assuming one lives long enough—seventy and eighty and ninety enter the realm of possibility, especially if one has known elderly parents or grandparents. My mother is ninety-four, relatively sound of mind but not of body, languishing in a nursing home in Minnesota and hating to be there. Visiting her is a traumatic experience for me, not only because I've had a slightly rocky relationship with my mother, but because seeing a panorama of white hair and wheelchairs and walkers makes me wonder when and if I'll reside in a similar place. The reality is that some of the other residents are no older than I am. It's not a bad place, but I wouldn't want to live there. My father avoided the experience by dying suddenly of a heart attack at age seventy while riding a mini-bike near his home. Perhaps this was a fortunate ending for my taciturn, enigmatic father.

Both of my grandfathers died relatively young, one of them before I was born. My maternal grandfather, Edward Uhl, died the year my mother graduated from high school. He died of a massive infection before the existence of antibiotics. My paternal grandfather, W.G. Marshall, was a shadowy figure with pale red hair reflecting his British ancestry, but perhaps that view comes from a picture of him now hanging in my bedroom hallway. I believe he died of heart failure when I was still very young. I never really knew him.

13

The women of the family seemed to live longer. Grandma Rosetta Hoffman Marshall, on the German side of the family, died of complications of Parkinson's disease in a nursing home in her late sixties. My view of Grandma as a hypochondriac who alienated her own sisters and lived almost as a recluse after her husband died is colored by my mother's dislike of her mother-in-law, whom she had to care for in the den-turned-sick room at the farm house before Grandma moved to the nursing home. I was away then, teaching in West Virginia, and when Grandma Marshall died, I was on my first trip to Europe. It was 1957.

I remember that Grandma Marshall was a good cook who always wore a white "housedress" when she cooked Thanksgiving dinner for the family soon after she'd moved to town. Her house on North Franklin Street in Whitewater, Wisconsin, had a spacious front porch with a wonderful glider that I liked to swing back and forth on while I watched the local 4th of July parade passing down the street to the city park. My brother John sometimes tried to share the glider with me, but we could never agree on how fast to swing. In fact, we couldn't agree on much of anything then, or for many years afterward.

I also remember the boxes of Whitman's Sampler chocolates we usually had on holidays at Grandma's. My addiction to chocolate probably began under Grandma's disapproving eye. I was the fat kid who could never stop at one chocolate. I still can't.

Grandma had a fascinating little ivory jewelry box in her bedroom, and I loved to explore it. Much later, I acquired a cameo pin and a gold bracelet and a sapphire ring and a garnet pin-and-earring set from that box. My niece Cindy has the box and a few of its other contents now. I still wear some of that old jewelry; its value is sentimental rather than monetary, but I wouldn't part with it.

Grandma Marshall spent her time visiting doctors about undiagnosed and possibly imaginary illnesses and crocheting doilies and lace tablecloths that my mother called "dust catchers." My mother tried not to show her dislike of her mother-in-law, but in later years I realized that Mother had never felt accepted by her in-laws. Perhaps she also envied Grandma Marshall for being the better cook. Like me, my mother wasn't especially interested in cooking, but since cooking was part of the traditional housewife's role, she tried.

My mother's mother, Minnie Louise Blanchard Uhl Pemberton Trezona, on the French side of the family, was widowed three times. Grandma Minnie, as we called her, lived to be eighty-nine years old. She died mostly of old age in a nursing home in Elizabeth, Illinois. By then, she was doubled over with a large "dowager's hump" on her back. She shared the family weight problem with my mother and me. She joked that she was the fattest woman in her nursing home. She occupied herself there by crocheting flowers, often in brilliant colors. She attached stems and leaves and sometimes sold her creations to visitors or donated them to charity. I still have five of her flowers, red, beige, and white, in my bedroom. The red flowers remind me of her spirit and cheerfulness.

When I first met Grandma Minnie, she seemed quite young and attractive, a free spirit who drove an old maroon-colored coupe with a rumble seat. I loved riding in the rumble seat, wearing sunglasses and a head scarf with the wind blowing my hair. I pretended that I was a glamorous movie star. I believe that Grandma Minnie had been widowed twice by that time. I knew only her third husband, William Trezona, whom we called "Grandpa Willie." Grandpa Willie smoked cigars and read western novels and rented a small farm near Scales Mound, in Joe Davies County in northwestern Illinois.

My paternal grandmother turned up her nose at Grandma Minnie and Grandpa Willie, seeming to consider them more or less the equivalent of trailer trash. My mother defended them, and to me, they were interesting. They lived

15

on a run-down farm with a ramshackle shed that actually collapsed one night while we were visiting. The house had no bathroom, running water, or electricity, things we'd always had on our farm. For several years, I actually thought it was fun to go outside to use the outhouse and to have a kerosene lamp with a tall chimney to light the way up the steep stairs to our bedrooms. Making the approximately one hundred mile trip from Wisconsin in one of our series of well-used cars was an adventure. My mother often wondered if the car was up to the trip, but I think we always made it without serious problems.

Grandma and Grandpa eventually moved into a small house in Scales Mound, with electric lights but still without plumbing. The path to the outhouse led through a large garden where Grandma grew all kinds of vegetables and flowers. After Grandpa Willie died, Grandma finally got a bathroom. By then I didn't enjoy visiting outhouses any longer, and I'm sure she didn't either. Poorly educated though she was, Grandma Minnie worked crossword puzzles successfully in ink, read romance and western novels, and crocheted practical things like dish cloths and potholders. She taught me to crochet too, but my interest soon waned. We all hated her habit of clearing the dirty dishes from the table and dunking them in the dishpan before we'd had a chance to finish eating.

Grandma Minnie had a hard life by today's standards, but she generally remained cheerful. I also think she began the career-woman trend in our family. Before she was married, she worked as a milliner in her future sister-in-law's hat shop. Much later, she worked at all kinds of jobs on and off the farm. I remember her selling home products door-to-door for a while.

Grandma Minnie eventually moved into a trailer on my Uncle Ed's farm in Elizabeth, Illinois, then to my mother's motel in northern Wisconsin, and finally back to Elizabeth until she entered the nursing home.

My stepfather, Merle Funston, whom my mother married long after I was grown and married myself, died after a fairly long struggle with emphysema. Seeing him hooked up to his oxygen tank and suffering was the best anti-smoking message I've ever known. However, his plight was nearly overshadowed by the fact that he had known how to live. He made my mother very happy for the few years they were married. Unlike my father, Merle was always ready for travel and adventure, and he had many, many friends. Unlike my Grandma Marshall, he seemed to suffer his final illness cheerfully and continue to tell stories of his earlier life.

As I think about the aging processes and deaths of my parents and grandparents, and of my stepfather, I am uncomfortably reminded of the inevitability of the whole process. Is it better to die early and/or unexpectedly, or to languish in a hospital or nursing home for years? Neither appeals to me, but what can I do? I can try to eat properly, exercise, and take care of my health, but perhaps more importantly, I can try to emulate the better qualities of my kin. Grandma Minnie's basic cheerfulness, no matter what the circumstances, was more attractive than Grandma Marshall's aloof melancholy. My stepfather's gregariousness and cheerfulness were more appealing than my father's alternating complaints and enigmatic silence.

I'll do the best I can to keep active as long as possible, trying to discover and appreciate the good rather than dwell on the unpleasant aspects of growing old. As Dylan Thomas advised, I'll try not to "Go gentle into that good night," but "Rage, rage against the dying of the light." And I'll try to do it cheerfully!

A Portrait of My Father

My father was an enigma. He was quiet and unde-monstrative. I never knew what he was thinking or feeling. There was usually an air of defeat about him. He was tall and thin and sort of gangly when he was young, plump and bald when he grew older. He had red hair, not as brilliant as the red childhood ringlets his mother, my grandmother, stored in a small white box in the dining room sideboard, but nevertheless red. There was a time when I wished for red hair rather than the common dark brown hair I shared with my mother and my brother. Father looked like his fa-ther, my grandfather W. G. Marshall, who died when I was a small child.

My father worked hard. He plowed and planted and milked cows and cleaned the barn and hauled cattle feed, sometimes with a hired hand and sometimes alone. He didn't seem happy. Family legend attributes that to his dis-appointment at having been forced to turn down an account-ing job in Minneapolis after college in order to run the fam-ily farm for his ailing father and his domineering mother. I don't know whether that was true or not. I don't remember ever having a conversation with my father about that or much of anything else. My mother was the dominant force in the family. My brother, who shares most of her traits, not our father's, nevertheless claims that Mother browbeat our father into submission and defeat, but I have never shared that opinion.

Father was a poor farm manager and never made much money. I know he had a good heart; he came to the rescue of a drunken friend and tried valiantly to keep him sober, with limited success. The man ultimately drank him-self to death, I believe. I don't think my father ever drank so much as a beer; his only vice was smoking cigarettes. His main form of recreation, as I remember, was hanging out at the farm implement dealer's shop in town. He checked out the machinery and observed repairs being made, but he said little. My mother considered this a waste of his time.

I remember a family trip to Northfield, Minnesota, home of my father's alma mater, St. Olaf College, when I was in the process of choosing a college. I expected to hear a lot about St. Olaf from my father, but as usual, my mother did most of the talking—at least that's how I remember it. I did not attend St. Olaf, nor did my brother, but much later, my brother taught and chaired the Chemistry Department there. I assume that Father was proud of him, but I don't remember his talking about it.

Father cherished his dog, Bill Beagle, for many years until Bill died of old age. During my mother's working years, my father ate (and sometimes shared with Bill) a very unbalanced diet, made up mostly of cereal and "store-bought" bakery goods, as he called them, with a pint of ice cream as a midnight snack. That diet probably contributed to his later heart disease, strokes, and Type II diabetes, as did his long-time smoking habit.

I remember my father's pride later when he was able to take me for a boat ride on Little Spider Lake in Woodruff, Wisconsin, where my parents ran the Edgewater Motel after they'd sold the farm. I was an adult by then, and still deathly afraid of water, but he talked me into the ride. He laughed because I wore the orange life jacket I always carried in the trunk of my car at that time. It was a rare father-daughter moment, but I don't remember any conversation. I remember that he enjoyed being with his grandchildren, my niece and nephew Cindy and John Marshall. They got boat rides too.

After having a major stroke, Father taught himself to read and write again, even though it was very difficult; stroke therapy, if any, was much more limited then than it is today, especially in small-town northern Wisconsin. His driver's license was revoked after a minor traffic accident, so he learned to ride a small motor scooter on a snowmobile path that paralleled the highway.

In 1974, at the age of seventy, my father, Clifford William Marshall, fell from his motor scooter onto the snowmobile trail, dead of a massive heart attack. My husband and I got the news at our hotel in London, England. There proved to be no affordable way to get to northern Wisconsin in time for the funeral, so we shared a small bottle of cognac in my father's memory. I comforted myself with the idea that my father would have wanted us to go on with our trip. At any rate, that's what we did. Fortunately, my brother was able to attend the funeral.

To me, my father remains an enigma. Perhaps he did manage to enjoy life in some way; I know that he and my mother traveled to Florida once or twice in their later years. My mother told me that he had enjoyed the sugar-free cookies I'd sent for his final Father's Day. That is the only gift I can remember giving him. Maybe he was even proud of my brother and me. Maybe under his quiet demeanor and his lack of communication, he knew some secret joy. My brother pities him as a victim of a dominating wife and a domineering mother, but I see him now as a victim of clinical depression that was never diagnosed or treated. I wish I'd had a chance to know him better—but perhaps I wasn't paying enough attention.

With my
Father and my
Mother, 1933

II. Teaching

Department Retirement Luncheon, 1999

After the CCCTU Banquet, 1999

A Writing Teacher's Confession, 1988

This essay was written in 1988 and published with the added afterword in Discourse, *a City Colleges of Chicago Publication, in 1991.*

In facing the problems and frustrations of teaching writing in a community college, new insights and approaches are possible even for a thirty-year veteran.

One of the in-class focused free writing assignments in an advanced Writing Across the Curriculum course I took recently was to react to a reading, the chapter "Writing from a Developmental Perspective" from *Learning to Write/Writing to Learn* by John Mayher, Gordon Pradl, and Nancy Lester (Boynton/Cook, 1983). Here, with very little editing, is what I scrawled on my yellow pad:

"One of the passages I marked in the assigned chapter is, 'It's possible to become a fully competent speaker, listener, reader, *and* writer without ever having heard terms like *noun* or *relative clause*, much less being able to identify or define them' (50). I learned the truth of this several years ago, so I was happy to be reminded of it again. When I last taught Basic Writing Skills, the lowest level of composition I've ever attempted, I assumed that I needed to begin by teaching the parts of speech, followed by phrases; clauses independent and dependent, adjective, adverb, and noun, restrictive and non-restrictive; simple sentences, compound sentences, and compound-complex sentences; then commas, semicolons, colons, apostrophes, question marks, quotation marks, spelling rules, and on and on. After I had taught my students all that a writer needed to know, I'd ask them to write a few short essays.

"The results of this approach were awful. For one thing, we barely got to writing at all. When we did, there was no correlation whatsoever between good grades on my grammar and sentence structure quizzes and good writing. I had foreign students who knew English grammar perfectly and got all A's on my quizzes, but couldn't or didn't write a single sentence in anything resembling correct, standard English. I had students who could write fairly well, as they could when they entered the class, but failed all my grammar, sentence structure, and punctuation quizzes. I had students who could do nothing. Most of the students showing early promise had dropped out long before the end of the semester, probably because of extreme boredom.

"Only as I began to analyze this fiasco did I realize that I hadn't relearned the fine points of dependent clauses, etc., until I began teaching composition, and that knowing about such things had nothing whatsoever to do with my own writing. I couldn't remember ever consciously looking for or trying to write a dependent adjective clause or a compound-complex sentence. As a matter of fact, I hadn't written much except comments on my students' papers for more than twenty years. What was I doing, anyway? No matter how logical and well-organized, my English 100 course was a disaster. After serious self-evaluation, my teaching changed dramatically."

An Afterword

My confession raises many questions: for example, if the parts of speech-phrases-clauses-sentences-punctuation-spelling-writing approach did not work, why not? What **does** work? Unfortunately, I have not discovered a magic formula for teaching writing, but no later class has been as disastrous as the one described above.

The change in my teaching approach has involved more writing of my own, increased flexibility and compassion, a growing awareness of recent composition theory and research, and continuing experimentation with everything from computers to writing-as-process to the free writing, brainstorming, student journal, and group projects of the "Writing to Learn" and "Writing Across the Curriculum" theorists. I'd like to have smaller classes and try an intensive conference-workshop approach, but that remains a dream.

Perhaps, as focused free writing is supposed to, my confession will encourage more answers through the future thinking, teaching, and writing of its author and its audience as well.

The Poet: A Poem from *Compupoem*

Soon after computers were introduced to the classroom, my students and I enjoyed playing with a computer program entitled Compupoem. *The exercise involved typing in a few nouns, verbs, adjectives, and adverbs that automatically became a poem. Here is a "poem" I wrote in 1986:*

The computer
  Powerful, competent
On the poet's desk
  Its cursor flashing, patiently
Awaits a human partner.

The poet
  Insightful, circumspect
In awe of technology
  Her fingers trembling, cautiously
Presses the compliant keys.

The poem
  Perceptive, eloquent
Across the magic screen
  Its words aglow, profoundly
Flows to greet posterity.

My Philosophy of Education, 1995

This statement was written at the request of the Wright College administration on the occasion of my being named Wright's Distinguished Service Professor for 1995-96.

My philosophy of education is based on the idea that students learn better and retain longer that which they are encouraged to discover for themselves. Even the most interesting lecture material presented by a skilled lecturer is lost on many students. Various kinds of small group work and sharing of ideas engage students' interest and lead to the kind of learning that will last beyond lecture notes and examinations. For example, if I ask my British Literature students to explain the events of Chaucer's "Wife of Bath's Tale," most will tell me that the Middle English language is too difficult; they don't understand. They ask me to explain the story in class. Instead, I assign a specific question to each group of two or three students and give them some time to come up with the answers. They do, and they share the answers with the rest of the class. The class can soon summarize the story in detail. A process of discovery has occurred, and the students will remember the tale better than if I had explained it to them.

I also believe that writing is the key to education: not only writing to display knowledge or literary talent, but writing to learn, writing to examine, writing to remember. Reading logs and/or journals are very useful in helping students remember what they have read, what they thought about it, what questions they would like the class to consider, and what topics they might use for later papers. Various in-class exercises in brainstorming and free writing enhance the learning process.

For example, early in one literature survey course, I asked the students to write for a few minutes about the most important or most interesting thing they had learned so far, and then share their papers with the class. The subject was nineteenth-century British literature. The responses varied

26

widely. One student said he had finally learned the real words to "Auld Lang Syne," a song he'd heard many times without comprehending what it was about. One older returning student wrote about her delight in discovering the poetry of William Wordsworth, a favorite of her son, an English major at a local university. Another student marveled that poetry was not as difficult as he had always thought. Yet another had learned that studying literature really requires quite a bit of reading time and effort. This exercise produced interesting and sometimes humorous responses, and proved useful for getting students to think and write and share.

Writing to learn can come in a computer word processing version also. As English composition students begin to compose in the computer classroom, I often ask them to write letters of thanks to the best teachers they have had, or letters of complaint to their worst teachers. As an alternative, I sometimes ask them to write letters to me, telling me what they have learned so far in my class, or what they are having problems with, or what grade they hope to earn. These assignments require thinking and organizing, in addition to providing valuable practice in word processing and spell-checking.

In short, my philosophy of education involves promoting student action and interaction, creative thinking and problem-solving, as opposed to the lecture and passive listener mode popular when I was a student.

In Defense of Poetry, 1996

This speech was presented at Wright College at the March 23, 1996, induction ceremony for new members of the Theta Omega Chapter of Phi Theta Kappa, an international honor society for students attending two-year colleges. It was published in the Spring 1996 issue of The Wright Side *literary magazine.*

Poets and poetry, especially poets and poetry from the past, are often considered irrelevant in today's society. Most of us, including college administrators, teachers, parents, and the scholars of Phi Theta Kappa, have to face practical problems: earning a living, providing for loved ones, helping to solve some of the immense economic and social problems that surround us. So what is poetry good for?

First, poets remind us of the unchanging problems and realities of society and human nature. Whether the subject of the poem be love or death or poverty, we can often say, "I understand; I've been in that situation myself." Secondly, poets help us deal with these realities, not by giving us pat solutions, but by offering inspiration, comfort, or escape, and by making us think.

"The world is too much with us; late and soon, / Getting and spending, we lay waste our powers." Those are the first two lines of a sonnet by British poet William Wordsworth, written about 1802. Wordsworth's theme is that his contemporaries did not appreciate nature, that they had "given [their] hearts away" to economic concerns. Somehow, that seems true today as well.

Poet John Keats, in one of his frequent melancholy moods, described some of his world's problems in the "Ode to a Nightingale" in 1819: he wrote that the nightingale has never known "The weariness, the fever, and the fret / Here where men sit and hear each other groan; / . . . Where but to think is to be full of sorrow." Today's pessimists, at least, would agree.

Another of the English Romantic poets, Percy Bysshe Shelley, was concerned with mutability or change. Nothing lasts: "Man's yesterday may ne'er be like his morrow; / Naught may endure but Mutability." Shelley also wrote, "The flower that smiles today / Tomorrow dies."

So far, I have shown that the nineteenth century British poets were a gloomy lot, and you may wonder why I would talk about weariness and sorrow and decay on this happy occasion. But no matter how pessimistic, the poetic lines I've read ring true and relate to life today as well as to life in nineteenth-century England. And fortunately, the same poets were visionaries too: while they couldn't solve the world's problems, they found inspiration and enlightenment in nature and the arts. We can do the same.

In "I Wandered Lonely as a Cloud," Wordsworth wrote of how he remembered a beautiful scene in a later moment of solitude: "And then my heart with pleasure fills / And dances with the daffodils." On returning to the picturesque ruins of Tintern Abbey in 1798, Wordsworth wrote that the beautiful sight created a mood "In which the heavy and the weary weight / Of all this unintelligible world, / is lightened . . ."

Keats wrote, in *Endymion*, "A thing of beauty is a joy forever." In "spite of despondence, of the inhuman dearth / Of noble natures, of the gloomy days," some "shape of beauty" such as the sun, the moon, trees or flowers "moves away the pall / From our dark spirits."

The poets show us that poetic inspiration, comfort, and escape come not only from nature, but from works of art as well. In his "Ode on a Grecian Urn," Keats provides an antidote to mutability: the young lovers pictured on the urn are not subject to aging and death: "More happy love! More happy, happy love! / For ever warm and still to be enjoy'd, / For ever panting and for ever young." To the beautiful work of art from antiquity Keats says, "When old age shall this generation waste, / Thou shalt remain, in midst of other woe / Than ours, a friend to man, to whom thou say'st / 'Beauty is truth, truth beauty,'—that is all / Ye know on earth, and all ye need to know."

I shall conclude with just a few more words from William Wordsworth: in his "Preface to *Lyrical Ballads*" in 1802, he wrote, "The man of science seeks truth as a remote and unknown benefactor; he cherishes and loves it in his solitude; the poet, singing a song in which all human beings join with him, rejoices in the presence of truth as our visible friend and hourly companion. . . . Poetry is the first and last of all knowledge—it is as immortal as the heart of man."

Laurence Perrine on "What is Poetry?"

In chapter one of *Sound and Sense: An Introduction to Poetry* (Harcourt, 4th ed., 1973), Laurence Perrine wrote, "Poetry is as universal as language and almost as ancient. The most primitive peoples have used it, and the most civilized have cultivated it. In all ages, and in all countries, poetry has been written—and eagerly read and listened to—by all kinds and conditions of people, by soldiers, statesmen, lawyers, farmers, doctors, scientists, clergymen, philosophers, kings, and queens. In all ages, it has been especially the concern of the educated, the intelligent, and the sensitive, and it has appealed, in its simpler forms, to the uneducated and to children. . . . It has been regarded as something central to each man's existence, something having unique value to the fully realized life, something that he is better off for having and spiritually impoverished without."

The Roads to Success: Wright College Commencement Address, Spring 1996

As I thought about speaking on this occasion, I realized that I had heard about thirty or forty commencement addresses in the course of my days as a student and teacher, and that I remembered none of those speeches well. I assume that the world leaders and Nobel and Pulitzer Prize winners who speak at some of this country's major colleges and universities, not to mention the actors, actresses, and other entertainers who sometimes speak, do say memorable things at commencements, and that many of the speeches I have heard undoubtedly conveyed interesting ideas. Still, I could not remember any specific examples.

One thing I did remember during my brainstorming process was that the speakers usually point out to graduating students that commencement is a beginning, not an ending. Then I asked myself, a beginning of what? What does graduation lead to? As I continued my search for a topic, I discovered, in the *Parade* magazine of the April 21 *Chicago Tribune*, a feature article entitled "The Key to My Success: Lessons from some of America's Most Successful Women," by Lauren Picker. I'd found my topic. Success, no matter how it is defined, is certainly the ultimate goal of every person graduating from Wright College today. The quest for success is what begins, or at least continues, today. What is success, and what are the different roads we, and especially you, the 1996 graduates of Wright College, can take to achieve it? Surely the four successful women quoted by Ms. Picker in her essay can provide useful hints to anyone going on to further education or to a new or enhanced career. I will also add a few suggestions of my own.

Mary-Claire King is the geneticist at the University of Washington in Seattle who demonstrated in 1990 that a single gene is responsible for early-onset breast cancer. She had struggled to confirm her hypothesis for seventeen years, with much of her work perceived as "nonsense" along the

31

way. Ms. King says that there are two keys to being creatively productive: "One is not being daunted by fear of failure. The second is sheer perseverance."

Rear Admiral Marsha Evans, who joined the Navy right out of college, is the first woman superintendent of the Naval Postgraduate School in Monterey, California. She has campaigned to open all ships and combat positions to all Navy personnel, regardless of sex, and has held positions once considered "for men only." Following a hazing incident at Annapolis in 1989, an earlier study Evans had done on the progress, or the lack of progress, of women at the Naval Academy was retrieved and considered, and women are now a key part of the brigade at the Academy. "Working hard overcomes a whole lot of other obstacles," Evans says. "You can have unbelievable intelligence, you can have connections, you can have opportunities fall out of the sky. But in the end, hard work is the true, enduring characteristic of successful people."

Ruth Simmons, president of Smith College, studied at Dillard University in New Orleans and at Harvard for a master's degree and a doctorate in romance languages. She is African-American, and such pursuits were very unusual for African-Americans at the time. She knew there was a good possibility that she would not be able to get a job in her field. Then, when she was asked to direct the African-American studies program at Princeton in 1985, she was told that accepting such a job would not be a good idea; she might be typecast in the academic world, thus ruining her career. Fortunately, she did not listen to such advice; she was convinced that there was important work to be done, and she brought in leading African-American teachers such as scholar Cornel West and novelist Toni Morrison. The African-American studies program became a model for other colleges. "Fear of failure is the fuel of achievement," Ms. Simmons says. "If you weren't afraid to fail, you probably wouldn't be highly motivated to work at the level that most of us have to work at to do well."

Simmons has also managed to combine family and career. In the past, her commitment to her children, including her insistence on picking up her young daughter from school every afternoon, caused her career to move slowly for a time, but she defends her priorities. Her advice? "It is possible when you are in your late 40's to take off in a career that's fabulous. The key is to maintain your skills. Make sure that you're constantly learning. When you're able, come into the workforce in a leadership role." Ms. Simmons has that role at Smith College.

Sally Fox is the founder of Natural Cotton Colours, a 2.5 million dollar business. Beginning as a hobbyist hand-spinner of cotton, she discovered and planted a handful of seeds for natural brown cotton and went on to become an ecological entrepreneur who created a new industry of natural fibers and fabrics that require no dyes. Her firm produces cotton in soft shades of brown and green for sheets, blankets, sweaters, upholstery, and more. Ms. Fox says, "You have to have a goal—and your goal has to continue to be updated. . . If you don't have a goal, you are just treading water. You have to know where you're going—or at least what you're intending."

Of course many similar stories about successful men have been written. In fact, men's success has generally been documented more often than women's, so I feel justified in emphasizing women today. But regardless of gender and re-gardless of whether the field of endeavor be science, the military, education, or business, these success stories have several messages in common: set goals and priorities; take risks; use fear of failure only as a motivator; work hard. The concept of hard work emerges from each story.

In case some of you think that these stories of very successful, pioneering women do not apply to you, or that their kinds of success are not the kinds you want or are likely to achieve, I will offer some further advice:

First, define success in your own personal way. Is it material goods like fancy houses or cars or clothes? Is it making a difference in the community, the nation, or the world by fighting for social justice or economic equality or peaceful relationships among nations? Is it finding the cure for a dread disease? Is it achieving admiration and fulfillment through outstanding achievements in a particular academic or scientific field? Is it inventing new machines or new technologies, or new ways to use the tools we already have? Is it family happiness, with healthy, happy children and grandchildren? Is it developing satisfying social relationships with those around you? Is it creative expression or self-fulfillment through literature or the arts? Is it the personal satisfaction of retreating from industrial society to commune with nature? Most likely, your definition of success will include bits and pieces of many of these things I have mentioned, and others as well. As Christopher Morley wrote, "There is only one success—to be able to spend your life in your own way."

Once you have defined success, determine what you will need to do to achieve that success. Find your own roads. Will success require more education? More work experience or training? A reordering of priorities or a plan for better use of your time? Decide what you need and what steps you will have to take to reach your goal.

Whatever kinds of success you are pursuing, I hope you will find that Wright College has provided a few tools to help you along the way. Of course you should have acquired a great deal of knowledge in your college courses, but there's more. If you have learned to organize your job and family responsibilities in order to get to your classes on time and get your assignments in on time; if you have learned to ask for help when you need it, but ultimately to depend upon yourself; if you have learned to work with and respect others, including those unlike yourself; if you have learned to analyze problems and employ critical thinking to solve them; if you have learned to read, write, and speak effectively; and most of all, if you have learned to work hard—you will be successful. This is indeed a new beginning. Define your own type of success, and follow your own roads as you seek it. Good luck!

Work cited:

Picker, Lauren. "'The Key to my Success': Lessons from Some of America's Most Successful Women." *Parade* 21 Apr. 1996: 4-5.

Marlys and Jules at Graduation, 1996

Farewell to Wright College, 1999: All We Need to Know . . .

In the 1990's, it was traditional for teachers retiring from the English Department to publish farewell messages in the department's magazine, The Wright Side. *As retiring department chair, I felt compelled to write an essay illustrating the typical English 101 format we tried to teach our students.*

A poster in my office reads, "All I need to know about life I learned from my cat." I have indeed learned a lot from my various cats during my long teaching career, but if I were to design a new poster, it would read, "All I need to know about life I learned by teaching English 101."

I learned a lot from my English 101 students. I remember a very tall potential basketball star at West Virginia University, where I taught for two years, who put his head down on my desk and cried after receiving an F on his first paper. I remember being astounded to discover that Joe could hardly read or write at all. I don't know the circumstances of his life, but poverty surrounded Morgantown, West Virginia. My idealism and my naïve belief that all students came to college prepared to do college work were shattered during my first week as a teacher. I learned compassion. I learned to admire teachers who could turn students like Joe into solid English 101 students.

I learned to appreciate and respect the amazing coping skills of my students. Many of them have been able to balance jobs, families, and personal problems with their college assignments and succeed. I learned to appreciate Wright College as a place where everyone has a chance, or several chances.

My students also taught me lessons on racism and ways to deal with it. I remember teaching an evening English 101 class at Wright during the early 1970's. My alphabetical seating chart put two handsome male students named Smith side-by-side. One was white, and the other was African American; they seemed suspicious of each other. They tended to take opposite sides in all class discussions, each trying to carve out a militant position for his race. By the end of the semester, both seemed to have mastered tolerance. Each seemed surprised to discover that the other was intelligent, articulate, and an excellent writer.

I recall Marcia, an English 101 student who took me up on my standing offer to let any student teach the class for one session; she did an excellent job. She and my other good students taught me humility. So did the students who were already computer experts when I introduced computers to my English 101 classes in 1985.

In addition to what I learned from my students, I learned a lot from my English 101 textbooks. Certain classic essays appear in almost every traditional English 101 collection: Maya Angelous's "Champion of the World," from *I Know Why the Caged Bird Sings*, for personal experience with profound social implications; E.B. White's "Once More to the Lake" for narration, description, nostalgia, and insights on social change, family relationships, and mortality; Bruce Catton's "Grant and Lee: a Study in Contrasts" for well-organized comparison/contrast and a taste of American history.

Through the years, I have often thought about an English 101 textbook essay entitled "The Mystery of Genius," the author of which I can no longer remember. I believe the main idea was something like "True genius is the ability to see patterns in things." Of course that is what the inventor or the research scientist does. That is how he or she envisions new technological marvels or discovers cures for diseases. Just this year, more than thirty years since I last encountered that essay, I again found myself telling my students that the "secret" of understanding any piece of writing is to look for patterns: repeated words, phrases, or ideas that take on greater and greater importance as they reappear. "If it's repeated, it must be significant. What does it add up to?" I have told my literature students the same thing to help in their quests for paper topics and theses: armor and weapons in *Beowulf,* the river and raft in *Huckleberry Finn.* Original? No. Over-simplification? Perhaps, but it works.

Yes, there is life after English 101, and that is my real point. I hope that my students remember their lessons as well as I remember mine, and that they go into the world practicing compassion, respect, tolerance, and humility. May they read, write, think, and live up to my high expectations of them.

At my Desk, 1999

III.Travel

On the California Coast, 1988

Copenhagen, Denmark, 1989

Mountain Memories, 1976

A slightly shorter version of this essay won third prize, a $25 gift certificate, in the Chicago Sun-Times Travel Readers' Forum *"Most Disappointing Travel Experience" contest, and was published on September 11, 1988.*

The view from the operating room was magnificent: fluffy white clouds just touching the snow-tinged mountain tops in early June, 1976. As I drifted toward unconsciousness, I heard the young intern, in his best school English, asking standard pre-operating questions: was I wearing contact lenses? A dental plate? He probably wanted to ask why an American woman my age was riding on a motorcycle, but he restrained himself. I wasn't able to answer any questions, my tongue thickened by anesthetic and my brain preferring to ignore this anticlimax to what was to have been a wonderful trip.

The place was Lienz, Austria. My husband, Jules, a Deputy U.S. Marshal, and I, a college English professor, both of us over forty, had dared to tour the Alps on a new BMW motorcycle, much to the amazement of friends and relatives. Jules wanted the excitement of a trip that would be really different, and he was convinced, by a minimum of riding experience, that motorcycling was the only way to travel. If I was a reluctant passenger, I tried not to show it.

The trip began ominously on a cold, rainy day in Munich. On the first day, we got lost and traveled on a narrow path ending in a flooded field. On the Grossglockner Highway, a bag fell off in an icy tunnel. Finally, on a sunny day, on a curving, scenic Austrian road, the trusty BMW left the road, and, as it fell, broke my right leg. Neither my husband nor the bike was injured.

When I awakened after the operation, the magnificent view was gone. I was in a corridor of a modest hospital, and no one around me spoke English. My leg was held together by three encircling wires, or so my husband told me, and it hurt.

Later, there was a room with another mountain view. For ten days I read and ate strange food and listened to what Mark Twain called "The Awful German Language," understanding not a word. I remember a helicopter hovering outside, apparently bringing in the victim of a mountaineering accident. I remember a mournful song about death, in English, played over and over on a phonograph in a nearby room. I remember Sunday night hymns echoing from the hospital lobby. Meanwhile, Jules toured Italy.

Finally, my leg in a cast from ankle to hip, Jules drove me in a rented Renault through Switzerland and back to Munich. Again, the scenery was lovely, but my major impressions were of pain and the indignity of falling flat on my back in a parking lot in Lucerne.

Was this "trip of a lifetime" a tragic nightmare? Is motorcycle touring best left to the young and daring? No! This vacation was filled with unique, if not entirely pleasant, experiences which made it worthwhile. As I look back to the trip, the mountain view from the operating room overshadows the pain.

Oh yes–we repeated the trip five years later, as older and more experienced motorcycle tourists. Through Germany, Austria, Italy, Switzerland, France, Liechtenstein– there is nothing like motorcycling to make anyone feel almost a part of the mountains. In 1983 and 1984 we returned again; once we lunched in Lienz and looked for the fateful curve in the road. As marvelous as those later trips were, I think that the first one is the one I'll always remember.

California Brewpub Diary, 1988

In summer, 1988, I managed to combine a motorcycle club vacation with writing. I wrote every day, recording our brewpub visits and observations. The observations were mainly my husband's; he was a former bar owner. I was not and am not a beer drinker, but I enjoyed exploring the brewpub culture that seemed to exist at the time. This essay was completed for a "Writing Across the Curriculum" course I took later in 1988.

Unfortunately, Sieben's River North brewery in Chicago, in which we were among many limited partners, failed, and we lost money along with everybody else. However, it was fun for a while. Brewpubs still exist, including Chicago's Goose Island Brewing Company, but not Siebens. We never had a chance to find out which of the California brewpubs mentioned here survived.

While other touring members of the Streeterville Scramblers Motorcycle Club searched for the most challenging mountain road, the most picturesque scenery, the coolest swimming pool, the best gourmet meal, or the biggest win at the gaming tables in nearby Nevada, my husband Jules and I visited California brewpubs. What better vacation activity for two Sieben's River North Brewery aficionados from Chicago in a state where the July-August 1988 *California Celebrator,* a "Beer News Brewspaper" published in Pleasanton, California, lists thirty-six brewpubs and restaurant breweries open or scheduled to open later in the year? We managed to visit eight establishments; we marveled at the variations in size, decor, and menus. The owners, bartenders, and brewmasters we met were friendly and courteous, and all had either heard of, read about, or visited Sieben's.

Tuesday, July 12, 1988: Since the tour began near San Francisco, our first stop was the San Francisco Brewing Company at 155 Columbus Avenue, established in 1985. A large brewing kettle is visible in a corner window, and the main room is a classic old-fashioned saloon on the site of the

Andromeda, built in 1907 and said to have been a showplace of its day. The saloon features a carved mahogany back bar, a long brass-trimmed mahogany plank bar with tile spittoon, and a series of eight pulley-operated palm fans with attached lights. The oak doors came from a waterfront saloon, the Albatross, for which the place was last named.

Tuesday is one of two weekly brewing days, so brewmaster Alec, who got his start in home brewing, with further training at the University of California at Davis, interrupted his cleaning operations to show us the rather small downstairs brewing area, not generally open for viewing, where he can brew approximately two hundred gallons per batch or six barrels at a time. Bartender Rick served us the featured brews, including Albatross Lager and Emperor Norton Lager. The menu announces snacks, salads, and sandwiches, as well as daily specials for lunch and dinner.

Wednesday, July 13: The Seacliff Café and Vest Pocket Brewery, 1801 Clement, is San Francisco's other entry on the *Celebrator* brewpub list, and it is a charming little blue-and-white American country-style café very different from the San Francisco Brewing Company. Owner-brewmaster Klaus Lang's idea is to "put the brew kettle back in the kitchen and restore fine beer to its rightful place next to fine food." The Seacliff features Anchor Brewing Company's Steam and Wheat beers and Old Foghorn Barleywine Ale, as well as Lange's own Seacliff Dutch Brown Ale, brewed only five gallons at a time.

Food is the main attraction here, with the right beer to accompany each dish. The menu features unusual items such as "Lamb Burger with Rosemary and Garlic Sauce" and "Ham and Leek 'Cocoons' with Swiss Fondue Sauce" as well as fish, seafood, "Old Fashioned Beef Stew," "Bratwurst with Red Cabbage Slaw and Mustard Sauce," and "Veal Shank braised in Dark Beer." "Special Blue-Plates by Whim or Season" are also offered. Unfortunately, we could not visit the Seacliff at lunch or dinner time, but Klaus Lange graciously opened his door to talk to us. We'll surely schedule lunch or dinner at the Seacliff on our next visit to San Francisco.

Thursday, July 14: On Thursday morning we headed for Calistoga, with a stop for Bastille Day festivities at the Domaine Chandon winery at Yountville in the Napa Valley. Later, at 1250 Lincoln Avenue in Calistoga, we found the Calistoga Inn restaurant, beer garden, and brewery and met owner Phil Rogers, who showed us his small, neat brewery in an historic building overlooking the beer garden. Good salads, sandwiches and various specials are served in the outdoor dining area. The featured beer is Calistoga Lager. Rogers visited Sieben's during the 1988 restaurant show in Chicago, and sent his greetings to Sieben's manager Laurel Hanson. He plans another Chicago visit soon.

Friday, July 15: As we rode toward Eureka, we saw the North Coast Brewing Company, 444 N. Main Street, Fort Bragg, a brewpub still under construction. Co-owner, general manager, and brewmaster Mark Ruedrich made his way through the sawdust to talk to us about his establishment, scheduled to open in late summer or early fall–as soon as the building and the beer are ready. The North Coast, conveniently located on Highway 1, is a huge place with a large parking lot, and it features a large, beautiful bar said to have been shipped "around the horn" for an earlier saloon. This bar rivals the San Francisco Brewing Company's in antique charm. We wished Ruedrich luck and put his place on our growing list of California brewpubs worth visiting.

Saturday, July 16: On our way from Eureka, California, to Coos Bay, Oregon, we stopped to peer into the windows of California's northernmost brewpub, the Humboldt Brewery at 856 10th Street in the small college town of Arcata, home of Humboldt State University. We were there hours before opening time, but the displayed photos of happy young patrons gave us some idea of the interior. According to an article by J. Dooley in the *California Celebrator*, Humboldt owner Mario Celotto (a former Oakland Raider) had to close his doors after his patrons consumed over 2400 gallons of beer during the first seven days of business, drinking the pub dry. That was in June, 1987. Humboldt's Oatmeal Stout won a gold medal at this year's Great American Beer Festival in Denver. Other products include Gold Rush Ale, Red Nectar Ale, Storm Center Porter, and Tooz's Golden Glow.

The decor features English beer pumps, large mirrors, pro football memorabilia, and windows that provide a view of tanks used in the brewing process. Historic photos from the area's pre-prohibition days are displayed in the dining area. The menu includes Buffalo wings, Cajon Burgers, Chainsaw Chili Burgers, and New Nectar Beer Sausages, as well as ribs, pasta, and weekly specials. The Humboldt is definitely a place to visit.

Wednesday, July 20: The Truckee Brewing Company is located in the Pizza Junction restaurant at 11401 Donner Pass Road in a shopping center in Truckee, not far from Lake Tahoe. Co-owner Steve Downing explained that he had a small brewing operation off the restaurant's main room, but he is not making beer there now. The Nevada City Brewing Company, which Downing also co-owns, supplies beer to Pizza Junction as well as to several Nevada City restaurants, and Pizza Junction also serves a large variety of bottled beers. The two red railroad cars which sit beside Pizza Junction, and undoubtedly suggested its name, may be used for brewing in the future. Steve and his partner, Gary Rausch, are kept busy by wall-to-wall weekend crowds at Pizza Junction, especially during the ski season, but they may put more emphasis on brewing later. The Nevada City brew and some accompanying garlic bread were excellent.

Steve Downing invited us to visit the Nevada City Brewery (not a brewpub) early Thursday morning, but the intense heat and some scheduling problems changed our plans. We'll try again next time.

Monday, July 25: After a few more brewless days (a fresh peach margarita was the special in the Josephine Room at the Gunn House in Sonora, where we stayed for three days), we found another brewpub on our way from Pismo Beach to Milbrae. The Monterey Brewing Company is located at 700 Cannery Row in a popular tourist area of Monterey amid T-shirt shops and other attractions. It is a busy place at lunch time. The brewing area is visible from the dining room. Both the indoor and the outdoor eating areas are small, and food is purchased at a counter. The simple menu includes hot dogs and corn dogs, and features a variety of sausages. Pale ale, amber ale, porter, and specialty beers in season are offered, as well as soft drinks for the younger tourists.

Monterey Brewing Company owner Tony Bindel is proud of opening his restaurant and brewery for under $100,000 and of making a profit immediately. Bindel expressed amazement at the scale and expense of larger operations, including Sieben's, which he'd read about.

Our final brewpub excursion on Monday evening took us to a much larger operation, the Tied House Café and Brewery at 954 Villa Street in Mountain View, south of San Francisco. A "Tied House" in England was a pub owned by a brewery and allowed to sell only the beer manufactured by that brewery, as opposed to a "Free House," which could purchase its beer from any distributor or more than one. Another Tied House is scheduled to open in San Jose later this year, and there may be more to come.

The Mountain View Tied House is a huge but attractive warehouse-like structure with an outdoor eating area, a rear indoor area with picnic tables, and a big dining room with many small tables. Part of the brewing area is visible through glass windows; the approximately ten huge stainless steel tanks suggest a great brewing capacity, but the courteous assistant manager on duty at the time of our visit wasn't able to tell us much about the brewing operation. An open kitchen allows patrons to see their food being prepared, and service seems to be friendly and efficient.

One interesting offering is the "Tied House Sampler." Three small glasses, one each of Tied House Pale, Tied House Amber, and Tied House Dark, are set in little circles on a mat containing a description of each beer, and the taster is advised to try the brews in the listed order. Tied House Amber was my favorite.

Our party of four enjoyed a "Brewer's Platter," a large, tasty assortment of smoked sausages and cheeses served with barbecued onion rings, pickles, and mustard. Other platters (servings for two or appetizers for four to six) are the smoked poultry and the smoked fish platters. The appetizer list also includes shrimp steamed in beer, oysters, red onion rings, calamari, and garlic bread with beer cheese. Various soups and salads are offered, as are side orders of barbecued red onion, whole roasted garlic, and French fries. Our friend Marty praised–and shared–the two-pound bucket of beer-steamed clams; Jules enjoyed the Cornish Pasty; friend Jim and I both ordered the special Reuben sandwich, which was excellent. Beer-mustard chicken breasts, burgers, and sausage sandwiches are also offered. Entrees include two choices from among sautéed fresh vegetables, barbecued red onion, wild rice pilaf, or French fries. We had no room for dessert, but the menu lists a cheese and fruit plate, fruit pie with cheese, and chocolate mousse.

Thus ended our California brewpub odyssey. Jim and Marty drove us back to our hotel (no, Jules didn't drink and ride). On Tuesday, we flew back to Chicago to end our two-week adventure. We returned with a long list of brewpubs to visit and revisit: the Devil Mountain Brewery at Walnut Creek with its award-winning Railroad Ale, Ironhorse Ale, and Devil's Brew; Buffalo Bill's Brewpub in Hayward; the brewpubs of Berkeley, Pasadena, Sacramento, San Jose, Santa Cruz . . . the list goes on. What about the beer? I am not a beer expert, so I can only say that, like the eight brewpubs we visited, it was interesting, varied, and always good. So were the imaginative names of the beers.

Motorcycling to the Soviet Union, 1990: *Tetris* Comes Alive

This essay was published in The Wright Side, *the Wright College literary magazine, in 1991.*

In the computer game *Tetris*, four-square pieces fall against backgrounds of colorful Soviet Union scenery. Summer in a park, a winter scene reminiscent of *Dr. Zhivago,* the Kremlin, a hockey arena, the ballet: the game's graphics portray a fantasy world I never expected to visit.

However, on July 5, 1990, my husband Jules and I embarked on our first trip to Eastern Europe: an Edelweiss Bike Travel Soviet Union tour. In its third year of conducting motorcycle tours to that area, the Austrian Edelweiss company led our group, forty-one at peak strength, plus two tour guides and an Intourist representative, on a trip that could only have been a dream before Glasnost and Peristroika. The group, on about thirty motorcycles, included seventeen Chicago-area Streeterville Scramblers Motorcycle Club members and guests; nine other Americans; eleven Germans; two Swiss; and two Britons.

After flying to Dusseldorf and then to Munich, we Americans journeyed to the Munich suburb of Sauerlach. We picked up BMW and Suzuki motorcycles, and on July 5, accompanied by a van and a trailer filled with luggage and spare parts, we headed for Vienna. There the European contingent joined us on an assortment of motorcycles including an Italian Moto Guzzi and an ancient British BSA. The next stop was Budapest, and finally, on July 8, we reached Ukraine.

First Impressions

Our first impressions of the Soviet Union involved delay, inefficiency, and filth. Crossing the border took nearly three hours; a border guard shift change and/or dinner break, just as the last two bikes remained to be processed, was responsible for about a third of the delay. While waiting, we observed an inbound Soviet car being pushed through the border crossing, as well as one being towed with a rope. The filthy, smelly rest rooms at the border were a shock: a shock that was to be repeated often before we left the country. Our impression was that we were in a country where many things just didn't work.

Once across the border, we noticed a long line of tiny, mostly battered cars waiting to cross into Hungary. Vacationers? Emigrants? Probably the former, but here and elsewhere we had the uncomfortable feeling that we didn't really know what was going on. As we moved on through Uzhgorod and Lvov in Ukraine; Brest and Minsk in Byelorussia: and Smolensk, Moscow, Novgorod, and Leningrad in the Russian Republic, the trip became a series of impresssions: things often difficult or impossible to understand, but always fascinating. I regretted the language barrier, and somehow everything I had ever heard about the "evil empire" haunted me.

Law and Order

We had been warned to stay on the approved Intourist route, and we saw uniformed men at major highway intersections. At one point our guide's request for a shortcut was denied by the police. From what we could gather, the problem was not secret military installations, but rather bad roads and a shortage of gasoline. Some of our faster riders were stopped for speeding, but the language barrier was at least as frustrating to the police as to the speeders. Some group members were fined a few rubles.

Soldiers and police were much in evidence in the cities, but most of these uniformed comrades, carrying briefcases, seemed to be going about their bureaucratic business, oblivious to tourists. The Moscow police controlled stoplights efficiently and unobtrusively from their raised lookout points and their cars as our group rode to the edge of Red Square for photographs near St. Basil's. Motorcycling is not allowed in Moscow, so the bikes were soon stowed in the Hotel Cosmos garage as we toured by bus, taxi, and subway.

On the Road

The roads were usually rough, dirty or muddy, and poorly maintained. In the cities, cobblestone streets, streetcar tracks as much as three or four inches higher or lower than the street surface, and manhole covers deeply imbedded or standing high all made motorcycling a challenge. Road and street repair crews seemed to work slowly, often with picks and shovels rather than high-tech equipment. We saw a street repair crew composed of two middle-aged, housedress-and-babushka-wearing women with shovels.

51

Cold and rainy weather, the scarcity of convenient rest stops and rest rooms, the lack of fairings (windshields) on most of the motorcycles: these were some other obstacles we faced. However, the only casualties were bruises and a broken collarbone. The latter gave the victim and the two American doctors in our group a chance to observe Soviet medicine at work: not bad, but somewhat different from ours. The van provided convenient rides for the injured.

The long lines at gasoline stations moved very slowly, and we noticed that gas was brought in not in huge tankers but in very small tanks on assorted dilapidated trucks. As tourists with expensive prepaid gas coupons, we often got special service, but gas stops for the group stretched on for an hour or more. Sometimes stations had no gas at all, so repeated stops and siphoning of gas between bikes were necessary.

We saw no auto or motorcycle repair shops. Here and there, usually near gas stations, we saw raised tracks with pits beneath for do-it-yourself auto repair. Another sign of the difficulties of driving was that drivers often removed their windshield wipers when they left their cars in hotel parking lots. Windshield wipers, like so many other things, were in short supply and apparently subject to theft.

Motorcycles of the kinds our group rode did not seem to exist in the Soviet Union, but battered old motorcycles with sidecars provided basic transportation outside the cities. We saw sidecars filled with hay, lumber, old tires, junk, and every other kind of cargo, not to mention family groups wedged in and wearing ancient helmets quite unlike ours.

The scenery was mainly unspectacular: mostly flat land or rolling hills, with the Carpathian Mountains of Ukraine providing some of the twisting roads motorcyclists like. Along certain roads, the country bus shelters were impressive: bright mosaics and beautiful designs showed that talented artists and crafts people had been at work in unlikely locations. Perhaps this should not have been surprising in a

country where the Moscow Subway features crystal chandeliers, paintings, mosaics, and statuary.

Large monuments were everywhere: tanks, planes, rockets, even an older Aeroflot passenger jet, protruded from gigantic platforms in parks and near the roads. The fortress at Brest, with its monument of a huge, scowling soldier's head overlooking the spot where Soviet soldiers held out against the Germans for six weeks during World War II, is an impressive sight.

Housing

Along the country roads, we saw everything from log cabins to charming cottages with carved "gingerbread" trim. We were told that some of the more picturesque dwellings were subsidized by the government as tourist stops. We were invited into one or two comfortable but not luxurious houses near the road; their residents were most charming and gracious. Boxlike city apartment buildings, even those still under construction, looked gray and forbidding: poor construction, the experts in our group scoffed. Balconies were often jammed with household goods, suggesting overcrowding.

Most of the hotels were comfortable, but the Planeta in Minsk featured a small sign near the reception desk proclaiming (in several languages) that there would be no hot water until August. At another hotel, the hot water was turned off at 10:00 p.m., and the all-night digging effort outside our window was apparently supposed to remedy the problem—eventually. Repairs, especially those related to plumbing, are not done quickly in the Soviet Union. Some of the hotels in Moscow and Leningrad, including Moscow's Cosmos and Leningrad's Pribaltiskaya, where we stayed, were quite large and luxurious.

Food and Drink

There were few places to eat lunch outside the cities. We laughed about lunch stops without lunch and coffee stops without coffee. Fortunately, we had been warned to bring assorted snack foods, so beef jerky, trail mix, candy, even peanut butter and crackers, were passed around. Our hotel breakfasts and dinners were adequate, but seldom gourmet fare. We did enjoy a luxurious lunch in Lvov, with everything from caviar to borscht to salad to meat and potatoes to dessert, for thirteen rubles each. The restaurant was beautifully decorated, with ornate carpets and chandeliers and draperies we didn't expect to see in the general Soviet grayness.

We were warned not to drink the water, especially in Leningrad, and we didn't. Bottled water, Pepsi, beer, wine, champagne, and vodka were the beverages of choice. Stolichnaya, sold for dollars, cost more than it does in Chicago, but sometimes cheap local vodka and champagne were available for rubles.

Shopping

For Soviet citizens, shopping must be tedious indeed. There seemed to be little merchandise of any kind available to the general public. Lines would suddenly form outside shops, but it was usually difficult to determine what was being sold. The line outside McDonalds in Moscow stretched for several long blocks, despite high prices and inclement weather. As our American newspapers have reported, the line at McDonalds was indeed far longer than the line at Lenin's Tomb in Red Square. In a shop somewhere, I noticed that purchases were added up on an abacus. In the GUM department store in Moscow, buying a compact disk recording of *Swan Lake* meant selecting the disk, waiting for the clerk to fill out a form, taking the form to an area next door, paying the required number of rubles, waiting for a receipt, and then taking the receipt back to the first counter to pick up the disk. Since the number of disks for sale was very limited anyway, perhaps this inefficient system didn't matter much.

In contrast, the hard currency shops in the larger hotels sold everything from Fuji film to Irish mineral water, and employed computerized cash registers. However, only tourists were admitted, and there was nothing to buy with rubles. Hard currency stores near the Pribaltiskaya in Leningrad offered sable coats, jewelry, and other expensive luxury goods to tourists. The salespeople seemed surly, perhaps because most of the items they sold to tourists were far beyond the reach of their personal budgets.

Black marketeers, the budding entrepreneurs of the Soviet Union, were everywhere. "Change Money?" was the most common query in a frantic quest for hard currency. There was no set exchange rate, and we were warned against black market transactions. Near every hotel and at every roadside stop, scheduled or unscheduled, young people appeared with bags of merchandise: nested matryushka dolls in every size, color, and quality imaginable; fake fur hats; vinyl army belts with buckles; mostly unauthentic military and police medals; cheap watches; Soviet flags; even an army coat. Those who enjoyed dealing may have struck some bargains (a few of which were confiscated at the border), but as a dedicated non-shopper even at home, I merely observed the scene. These black market activities were illegal, yet so obvious that the authorities must have deliberately looked the other way.

Impressions of Moscow

Moscow, capital of the Soviet Union and of the Russian Republic as well, is a cosmopolitan city of nearly nine million residents. The most impressive and most photographed building on Red Square is the Cathedral of St. Basil the Blessed, also known as the Cathedral of the Intercession or Pokrovsky Cathedral or just St. Basil's. Built in 1555-60 on the orders of Ivan the Terrible and now a museum, it is a combination of nine churches, each with its ornate, multicolored dome. St. Basil's presents an interesting contrast to the relatively unadorned Lenin Mausoleum nearby.

The Kremlin (fortress or citadel) features massive walls, ornate towers, palaces, and its own cathedral square with an array of golden onion-shaped domes, as well as the major government buildings. The Armory Museum of the Kremlin contains a large collection of arms and armor from Russia and abroad; magnificent gold and silver objects, many of them gifts to the czars; and the thrones, crowns, robes, and carriages of pre-revolutionary days.

The Novodevichy Convent, the subway, the Bolshoi Theatre, the sports center: there are more things to see in Moscow than can be absorbed in one visit. A night at the Moscow Circus was especially memorable. The circus featured skilled and enthusiastic performers; its most unusual feature was a water ballet presented in a large tank or pool that was raised to replace the ring.

Leningrad, "Venice of the North"

Even in the rain, the former St. Petersburg, built partially on islands and featuring many bridges, is an impressive combination of western European and Russian architecture and art. The Hermitage is a maze-like complex deserving far more time than we spent there. Here the wealth of the nobility and the merchants and the treasures of the czars are on display. Leonardo, Raphael, Michelangelo, Titian, El Greco, Van Dyck, Rubens, Rembrandt: all are represented here in a setting of rich marble, malachite, jasper, and agate. St. Isaac's Cathedral, largest church in the city and now a museum, features a gilded dome, marble walls, and columns of lapis lazuli and malachite.

Russia means ballet, and although major Russian ballet companies and their superstars, like ours, vacation in the summer, we were able to see *Swan Lake*. The Cultural Centre of Intourist is not the Kirov or the Bolshoi, but we saw an excellent performance by potential stars of the future.

The People

What about the Soviet people? Unfortunately, we did not get to know or understand them well. However, we formed a few impressions. Our Intourist guide was eager to call himself a Ukranian, not a Russian, and was proud of his family and the home he was building in Uzhgorod. He smoked constantly, as did many of his compatriots, despite the shortage of cigarettes. He seemed curious but not especially optimistic about what recent political and economic changes would bring. Our occasional local tour guides, often attractive young women, spoke English well and did their jobs well, but they smiled little and admitted to being very poorly paid by our standards.

A woman generously offered us some of the raspberries she was picking beside the road. A Russian teacher of English leading her charges on a field trip was eager to talk to us and told us a bit about her village. A member of our group gave her a copy of *Vogue* magazine; I wonder if conflicting views of American women as grubby motorcyclists and as wearers of elegant fashions confused her. The children, like children everywhere, were friendly and curious. They liked gifts of chewing gum and ballpoint pens, and they were fascinated by the motorcycles. Some even accepted short rides. Many knew some English.

Religion appears to be making a comeback. Fortunately most of the beautiful cathedrals were preserved as museums rather than destroyed by war or atheism. We observed several cathedral weddings, and we were told of services held recently in some of the cathedrals we visited.

Final Impressions

From Leningrad, we rode to the border and, after a long, rain-soaked delay with much baggage searching, crossed into Finland. Immediately the countryside looked greener, the roads were clean and well-paved, the cars looked better. We felt that we had arrived in a country where things worked. Despite very high prices, we enjoyed a brief stay in Helsinki and then traveled back to Germany via a nearly twenty-four hour ferry ride. Next, we rode on to Hannover and Sauerlach, to fly back to Chicago on July 24.

Tourists rarely learn enough about the countries they visit, and we certainly did not. Our Soviet Union tour was an interesting, challenging adventure that left us curious about the country's future. The realities of *Tetris* and the Soviet Union still remain elusive.

Postscript: August, 1991

A coup, tanks in the streets of Moscow, the citizens' resistance, the return of Mikhail Gorbachev and his resignation from the Communist Party, the increasing power of Boris Yeltsin, declarations of independence by the Baltic republics and Ukraine: all these recent events kept me near a television set with a curiosity intensified by my visit to the Soviet Union little more than a year ago. With every picture of St. Basil's, Red Square, or the Kremlin walls, I could say, "I was there!"

Of course last year's trip did not enable me to predict this year's dramatic events, but I left the Soviet Union believing that change was inevitable. How happy I am that the coup brought no bloody massacre, and that the changes promise to be peaceful ones. Perhaps I can return some day to visit a people enjoying better living conditions and the freedom so many fought for in the streets of Moscow.

On the Road

Panama Canal Cruise, Cunard Princess

Alaska Cruise, S. S. Universe

Impressions from Seven Continents

I grew up with an ever-increasing mental list of the world's wonders, both natural and man-made, that I wanted to see. My dreams began with Anne Hathaway's cottage, inspired by the needlepoint picture my mother completed as she awaited my birth; the ruins of Pompeii, inspired by my reading of *The Last Days of Pompeii*; Rome's Coliseum, inspired by research for a high school paper I wrote entitled, "The Coliseum as a Symbol of Rome"; and on and on. The more I read, the more movies I saw, and later, the more TV shows I watched, the longer the list grew.

My ancestors had reached the United States long before I was born, and travel was rare in those days, except for the wealthy. I knew no travelers. My real world as I grew up was the American Midwest: Wisconsin, Illinois, Iowa, and Minnesota. I don't remember leaving the Midwest until I began my two-year teaching job at West Virginia University in 1956. However, my ever-expanding fantasy world eventually extended to all of the seven continents. By the end of 2005, that world had, in a sense, become reality. I had visited all the continents.

As I look back at my travels, I realize that giving a full account of each trip would be impossible. Each trip was wonderful in its own way, but they now tend to overlap in my mind. Perhaps I can best describe my travel adventures through a few of the impressions that still linger as vivid memories, no matter how much time has passed.

Of course North America was my first continent. Once I left the Midwest, I saw the Statue of Liberty, the Empire State Building, the Liberty Bell, Colonial Williamsburg, and the eastern and western mountains. The Grand Canyon, most of the national parks, and Las Vegas were also among the many impressive features of our country that I visited, some more than once. I remember saying that one visit to Las Vegas was enough, but in reality, I have returned there many times. Friends moved there. Motorcycle trips began there. My flights from Chicago to visit my brother in south-western Utah ended and began there. There's no escaping Las Vegas. I eventually visited Alaska and Hawaii too, and marveled at Mt. McKinley and the Pearl Harbor monument, among other wonders.

In Canada, I specifically remember the Chateau Frontenac in Quebec City. I saw it as I began my first trip to Europe in 1957, when our small ship sailed through the St. Lawrence Seaway on its way to the rough North Atlantic Ocean and on to England. Much later, I was impressed by Lake Louise and many other natural and man-made sights throughout the various provinces of Canada. Jules and I also visited Mexico briefly, as well as the Central American countries of Panama and Costa Rica on later trips. Our Panama Canal cruise was fascinating because of the man-made wonders of the canal itself. I also remember the locks and the ships from all over the world.

My 1957 trip to Europe, the first of many, featured my first visit to Anne Hathaway's cottage, my earliest fantasy of escape and peaceful beauty. I also saw Westminster Abbey and the Houses of Parliament and the Tower of London and the highlands of Scotland and Edinburgh Castle, as well as Loch Ness (without the monster). I took a side trip to Paris to see the Eiffel Tower and to Amsterdam to see the canals, assuming that this would be my one chance to see them. Two other members of our larger Experiment in International Living group joined me, apparently feeling as I did. At that time, the thought of more than one trip to Europe just didn't cross my mind. I was only 25, so the possibility that I would still be traveling , or even still alive, nearly fifty years later just did not exist. I remember a few small things from that trip: struggling to ride a bicycle up hills in the highlands (I was no athlete even when I was young), walking down Edinburgh's Royal Mile from the castle to Holyrood House on a beautiful day, Edinburgh's huge floral clock, the cleaning women in Amsterdam actually wearing wooden shoes while they worked.

At Anne Hathaway's Cottage, 1957

Between 1957 and 1974, I was busy finishing my education, establishing my teaching career, marrying, divorcing, remarrying, and saving money. Then it was time to go back to England with my husband Jules to revisit some of the same places. I especially remember sailing home on the Queen Elizabeth II. It was then that I vowed to have an outside cabin on any future cruises, but the ship was magnificent.

Our five European motorcycle trips began in 1976. On the first trip, I broke my leg in a fall from the bike outside Lienz, Austria, and missed much of the tour (see "Mountain Memories," page 41). I insisted on going back, and the other Alpine trips in 1981, 1983, and 1984 were less traumatic. Germany, Austria, Switzerland, Lichtenstein, France, northern Italy: motorcyclists love riding in the Alps. I was often terrified, but I enjoyed the trips anyway.

I remember the sounds of cowbells from the pasture behind our small ski lodge somewhere in Switzerland. I remember Munich's Hoffbrau House and Glockenspiel. I remember a wine and cheese lunch with my husband in our hotel room somewhere, with a lovely waterfall outside as background music. That was more romantic than lunch at any restaurant could be. I remember watching a BMW motorcycle TV promotion in Italy, featuring our tour group riding along. I remember thinking that all motorcyclists in full riding gear and helmets look alike, and that we could have been anyone. Even the motorcycles looked alike, but I remembered the cameras and knew that it was our group.

On the fifth trip, in 1990, we began in Munich and rode east through Austria and Hungary and into Russia. That trip deserved to be commemorated in a long article, and I wrote one (see page 49). That was my last long motorcycle tour; then arthritis made riding too painful. Of course there were many motorcycle trips in the United States and Canada between 1976 and 1990, and Jules kept riding through 1999. We took other trips during that time as well, without the motorcycle. In 1985, I returned to England to take a summer course in poetry at Cambridge University, and my mother went with me. It was her first and only trip abroad. I returned alone in 1989 for another class. After 1990, I kept traveling, but never again by motorcycle.

Together, Jules and I saw Greece and Spain and Portugal and Norway and Sweden and Denmark. I'll always remember struggling up the hill to the Parthenon in Athens. The story of the missing Elgin marbles influenced me to return to London the following December to see them at the British Museum. They were worth the trip, as was the Parthenon. I remember hating the thick air pollution in Athens; it seemed so out of place among the beautiful once-white monuments. The ruins of Ephesus in Turkey were memorable, too.

I remember the bullring in Madrid (no bullfighting for me, though), the Alhambra, the gigantic Rock of Gibraltar looming ahead as we approached by bus, and the Barbary Apes we saw there, and Spain's Costa del Sol, where our hotel room overlooked a magnificent beach. I remember Norway's fiords and the North Cape, Copenhagen's waterfront and Tivoli Gardens, and a hydrofoil ride from Copenhagen to Malmö, Sweden.

We returned to Italy in winter, 1995-96. Our motorcycle trips had usually included northern Italy; we'd visited Venice several times, but this time we found it flooded, with wooden walkways the only way to navigate St. Mark's Square. My main goal on that trip was to see Rome, with its Coliseum, and later, the Leaning Tower of Pisa.

Rome fulfilled my expectations. Even though I am not Catholic, there was a certain thrill in listening to (but not understanding) Pope John Paul II's New Years Day address from high up above St. Peter's Square. I remember remarking that the tiny figure in the window many stories up could have been anyone or no one, for all we could see, but the huge crowd was obviously thrilled.

Michelangelo's glorious ceiling in the Vatican's Sistine Chapel is breathtaking! So is his statue, *David,* in Florence, which I also saw on that trip. Somehow visions of Michelangelo's art remain very vivid in my mind. Both the ceiling and the statue are amazing artistic feats, larger than life and unforgettable. Of all the works of art I've seen, only the Louvre's *Mona Lisa, Venus de Milo,* and *Winged Victory* seem equally memorable.

The Coliseum, even on a gray day, also fulfilled my expectations from my high school days. It seemed even larger than I'd imagined, and it brought stories and movies about chariot races and gladiators to life. I remember a long walk from our hotel to the Spanish Steps and sitting near the top of the steps, too tired to walk down and then back up. Of course there is much more to see in Rome as well, and I plan to return in 2006.

The Leaning Tower of Pisa was swathed in scaffolding, but otherwise it looked as it looks in photographs. It is a strange phenomenon indeed.

The Spain and Portugal trip included a brief visit to Tangier, Morocco, our only visit to the African continent together. Our last joint trip to a "new" continent was to Oceania (Australia, New Zealand, and Fiji) in 1998. That trip inspired a photo exhibit we held at Wright College, a few photos from which now hang on the walls of my condo.

A Tree at Ayers Rock

Our trip began in the Outback. Alice Springs is no longer the frontier outpost I'd seen in old movies, but quite a modern town. From there we saw Simpson's Gap and Standley Chasm, and then we went on to Ayers Rock and the Olgas Mountain Range. Ayers Rock is one of the most impressive natural wonders I've ever seen, gleaming different shades of red depending upon the light and the time of day. I can see why this is a sacred place to the Aborigines who believe in its powers. We flew back to Cairns, and then traveled on to Port Douglas and the Outer Barrier coral cay, from which we could explore the Great Barrier Reef.

I'll always remember the coral and the fish of the reef, seen through the glass sides and bottom of a sort of miniature submarine. We watched the divers from an observation area, but we were not able to join them. Not only were we old, but I couldn't swim and was afraid of water. The birds, the kangaroos, the rain forests, the emus, even the butterflies in Australia are interesting. The Sydney Opera House is perhaps the country's best-known man-made wonder, and it was a thrill to see it not only from the inside but from a harbor cruise view of the exterior. Bondi Beach, the Botanic Gardens, the Olympic Park then being built for the 2000 Olympics: there's no end of wonderful things to see in Australia. I wish we could have stayed longer.

Then it was on to New Zealand. I loved Christchurch, probably because it's so English, with its colonial Victorian architecture. A visit to Queenstown brought a side trip to the Walter Peak sheep station and a demonstration of sheepdogs at work. We toured Milford Sound, Kipling's "Eighth Wonder of the World." I remember that Jules and I took a scenic flight back to Queenstown in a small airplane, and it was a "white-knuckle flight" all the way. For all my travels, I've always been afraid of small airplanes, and as the little plane circled round and round to get up over the cliffs and peaks, I was sure we wouldn't make it. However, we did. I didn't stop shaking for quite a while!

On to the North Island of New Zealand: Auckland and its harbor are beautiful, and I still remember Kelly Tarlton's Underwater World, where we felt as though we were inside a huge aquarium. I remember some scary sharks swimming above my head, as well as more species of aquatic life than I'd ever seen. We went to Rotorura, heart of the ancient Maori culture. We saw bubbling mud, geysers, and natural steam vents, as well as an arts and crafts center and a traditional concert.

My main impressions of Fiji are of the difficult, inefficient customs process, the poverty in the area, the heat, and the impressive seaside resort where we relaxed before flying home. Some people love to bask in the sun on tropical islands, but I don't. All in all, though, this was one of the best trips Jules and I took together. Oceania (Australia) is very, very far away, but everyone should go there if at all possible.

With three continents left to visit when Jules died in 2000, I had to decide whether to go on traveling, alone, or to end my seven-continent quest. By this time, my physical health and my agility were somewhat in question, but I chose to go on. Jules had never been interested in going to Asia, so China and Thailand were my first solo destinations. Jules and I had traveled most recently with Grand Circle Travel, so in 2001, I joined one of their groups as a solo traveler. I have continued to travel with Grand Circle ever since.

I flew first to Tokyo, so I guess I've technically been to Japan, even though I did not leave the airport. The China trip was impressive from beginning to end. The emerging wealth and the contrast between rich and poor in the cities were evident. The ugly air conditioning units and TV satellite dishes haphazardly attached everywhere on large city apartment buildings seemed to turn them into instant slums. The Great Wall seemed to go on and on, snaking through the countryside.

From the Yangtze River cruise, I could see marks high up on the cliffs indicating the future height of the water when the Three Gorges Dam is finished. It was obvious that some villages and some history would be submerged. The dam itself was a huge marvel of engineering, even in its unfinished state, and a model was nearby to show us the scope of the finished dam. I don't believe that the dam is finished yet, and I hope its advantages outweigh the disadvantages of burying part of a culture. The Yangtze is obviously an important part of Chinese commerce. We saw every type of commodity being transported by boat.

Of course Tiananmen Square brought memories of what had happened there, and a large portrait of Chairman Mao still hung prominently on a nearby wall. Later, we saw chained prisoners being transported at gunpoint in the bed of a truck. I wished I could have known what was going on; I later heard a rumor that the prisoners were on their way to execution for relatively minor crimes, but our tour guide would not speak about it. Traveling without understanding any languages other than English has its drawbacks, as I've long known. We saw the amazing Terra Cotta Warriors and some magnificent scenery, and I learned a bit about the country's history. However, I wish I could have talked to the ordinary citizens. I've felt that way in many countries.

Thailand epitomized tropical beauty and economic contrasts. The magnificent temples covered in brilliant gold leaf made me wonder how the people of a relatively poor country could have afforded such extravagance; we were told that many ordinary people had contributed what they could. According to our guide, the people of Thailand do not like to be reminded of *Anna and the King of Siam* or its view of their earlier society. I loved the movie, but I see their point.

I didn't travel in 2002; I needed time to recover from my move from house to condo, the 9/11 terrorist attack trauma, and the broken pelvis I suffered in October, 2001, in a fall. But by 2003, I was ready for a cruise on the Danube: Eastern Europe to the Black Sea. I had visited Budapest before, but I added Bucharest, Romania, and Belgrade, Serbia/Montenegro, to my list of cities. All three are interesting, but somehow, the countries that made up the former Yugoslavia did not become separate entities in my mind. Apparently some citizens felt nostalgia for the former Communist governments that provided them with secure jobs, while others welcomed more freedom and the chance to be entrepreneurs. Some were doing well; others weren't.

The water in the Danube was very low in summer, 2003, and our small ship couldn't make it all the way to the Black Sea. However, we traveled by private train from Bucharest to the coast and finally reached the Black Sea. I know that I enjoyed this trip, but somehow I have fewer memories of it than of some of the others. I did learn that the Danube is often not very blue, but it does pass some magnificent scenery.

By 2004, I was ready to see another part of Asia, Israel, and another part of Africa, Egypt. It had always surprised me that Jules, with his Jewish background, had no desire to visit Israel. Of course the constant wars and political upheavals over the years had been discouraging, but by 2004, conditions seemed to have calmed down, at least temporarily. I had no special religious ties to the Holy Land, but I had read the Bible, and I wanted to see Jerusalem, with its Wailing Wall; the Garden of Gethsemane; the Sea of Galilee; the Dead Sea; even the ugly walls and fences then being built to wall off the Palestinians. Our tour group was always accompanied by armed guards, and we toured the country without incident.

Several vivid impressions of Israel remain. I remember the whiteness of Jerusalem's buildings and the tombs outside the city, as seen from the Mount of Olives, as well as the reverence shown at the Wailing Wall. I admired the fact that Jews, Christians, and Arabs managed to live together in the city itself fairly harmoniously, no matter the disputes elsewhere. I regretted that we could not visit Bethlehem, apparently because it was under Palestinian control, and/or because of damage done by Israeli attacks. Israel was another country where I was not always sure what was going on.

I wondered at the conflicting accounts of the locations of the Stations of the Cross and the site of the crucifixion. Some religions seem to make these things seem so definite. I remember the twenty-something daughter of our Israeli tour guide coming to our hotel to visit her father. She was in the army, and she was wearing camouflage gear and carrying a large rifle. We were told that being armed at all times was a requirement for members of the military services. Of course I believe in equal opportunity, but somehow, seeing this young, beautiful girl with a rifle in a luxurious, peaceful hotel lobby seemed incongruous.

To me, Egypt was an exotic and mysterious country, site of the Pyramids and the Sphinx, which had long been on my fantasy list of things to see. Everything in Egypt lived up to my expectations or surpassed them. I was especially impressed by Abu Simbel. I had read of the raising of the temples to keep them safe from rising waters after the building of the Aswan Dam, and I was surprised to see that the huge statues and the temples looked as though they had always been exactly where they were. This project surely combined ancient and modern engineering expertise. The tombs in the Valley of the Kings, Luxor, and the many other temples were like nothing I'd seen before, and cruising the Nile revealed many interesting sights, far more than I can remember or describe here. I remember wonderful Cairo and the former palace-turned-hotel where we stayed. I remember the women sitting near an outdoor tented dining area making and baking in a small clay oven the pita bread we would actually eat that night. I remember a dinner on a boat moored on the Nile from which we could marvel at the lights of Cairo at night, as well as the many boats that passed by.

I was impressed by a factory that produced paintings on papyrus, depicting ancient Egyptian scenes, and I bought a large one to hang above my fireplace, as well as several smaller ones. Fortunately, they could be rolled up and stuffed into my overflowing suitcase. I had them framed in Chicago. I also couldn't resist a gold cartouche, specially made with my first name in hieroglyphics. The letter M is represented by an owl! I can't vouch for the authenticity of the hieroglyphics, but the cartouche is lovely.

Since tourism is the main industry in Egypt, I wondered how the country could survive: so much history, so many sights to see, but what of the future? Our tour bus was usually followed by a vehicle filled with armed guards; since tourists were killed at Luxor a few years earlier, there has been a strong effort to bring more of us back to visit, safely.

At Abu Simbel

By 2005, I still had two continents left to visit, South America and Antarctica. I had thought that Antarctica, especially, would be too difficult for a seventy-two year old with bad knees. I'd seen pictures of the Zodiac rafts that tourists had to take from the ship to the mainland, and I wondered how I could possibly get into and out of one. I'd heard tales of life at the remote American research stations and the terrible isolation there. I had not seen *March of the Penguins* yet. But in January, summer in Antarctica, I set out for an Antarctic Peninsula cruise on the *Marco Polo.* The trip began in Argentina, so I would see my last two continents in one trip!

Buenos Aires made me think of Evita and beef and the tango. The weather was hot, and our time there was short. Still, I remember the city square and the palace balcony from which Eva Peron addressed the crowds, as well as her family tomb in the huge old cemetery. We saw beautifully-dressed tango dancers and the former "red light district" which is now a restored tourist attraction, still picturesque. The small amount of Argentinean beef I ate was too tough, but I never went hungry.

From Buenos Aires, we flew to Ushuaia, Argentina, southernmost city in the world, the usual setting-off point for Antarctica. Nestled against the Andes Mountains, Ushuaia truly seems like the end of the world. We navigated the turbulent Drake Passage and set out for the Antarctic Peninsula. The *Marco Polo* is a comfortable ocean cruise ship, and my single cabin was more than adequate. The voyage included red parkas for all, and we had been asked to bring boots. I'd find out why later.

The ship was staffed with explorers and scientists, experts on the flora and fauna of Antarctica. There were interesting films (including *Shackleton*) and lectures, and I learned a lot. One of the most fascinating things I learned was that no country "owns" Antarctica; there is an agreement that all countries will share the right to do research there, and that no one will be permitted to pollute or exploit the land. Dropping Coke cans and potato chip bags is a no-no, as is interfering with the lives of the penguins and other wildlife. Respectable tour companies follow the rules; I hope everyone does.

Zodiac cruises to the shore depend upon the weather; if the seas are too rough, passengers stay aboard the ship. We were lucky, however. We had four or five shore excursions. We saw Adele and Gentoo and Chinstrap penguins. They are all smaller than the magnificent Emperor penguins portrayed in *March of the Penguins*, but in many ways, they look the same: tuxedo-clad, dignified, even inquisitive.

I found out that I was not the only person who needed to be helped into and out of the Zodiac, and I was helped. Getting ashore was difficult, but possible. Remember the boots? We needed them for the same reason that a farmer needs to wear boots in the barnyard. "Penguin droppings" were everywhere, and the smell was distinctive. The ship's crew always washed off our boots before we returned to the Zodiacs for the trip back.

I took my first steps on Antarctic territory at Water-boat Point, the site of the Chilean Videla Research Station. There were penguins everywhere, close enough to touch if we had been allowed to, and if we had been able to leave the walkways. The mostly Gentoo penguins nest in every nook and cranny, and walk about proudly, probably curious to learn about American tourists.

The Antarctic scenery is magnificent, and the weather not nearly as cold as one would expect in that vast whiteness. I remember a sunny day on the ship when we could take off our heavy parkas and bask in the sun on the deck for a while. After all, it was summer. We saw a para sailor hovering over our ship, his colorful parachute quite a contrast to the blue sky and the white, icy background. No place could be more beautiful.

We had some rough seas, some rain, and some sea-sickness (I was lucky enough not to get seasick), and we left Ushuaia for Buenos Aires and then home on first a rainy and then a very hot day. But it was, indeed, another trip of a life-time.

Me→

Although I rarely took two long trips in the same year, I suffered from my usual fears that my health would suddenly deteriorate and my travel career would end. I was still ready for another exotic, far-away Asian country: India. I went there in late September, 2005. I think my interest came partly because my doctor and her doctor-husband are Indian, as are so many Chicago doctors and other medical personnel, and partly because I'd read so much about the outsourcing of call centers and similar jobs to India and about the high educational level and improving economy there. Of course, there was also the Taj Mahal, one of the remaining "must sees" still on my list. The weather was hot and the trip arduous, but as usual, it was wonderful. We started in Bombay. I remember the strange coincidence of riding to the airport in a taxi driven by a native of Bombay; he told me how wonderful, but crowded, his home city was. Of course he was right.

I remember a boat trip in the rain to Elephanta Island, where I faced the indignity of having to be carried in a chair with four poles by four skinny, barefoot men up the steep hill to the caves because I have great difficulty climbing both hills and stairs. Of course I wasn't the only one who needed this rather inexpensive service, but I never want to be reminded that I'm not young and agile any more. The sculpture-filled caves were worth the indignity.

I'll always remember the crowded streets of Delhi, full of cars, busses, trucks, camels, rickshaws, bicycles, and people, people, people. Sacred cows? A few, but the authorities have apparently relocated most of them to less congested areas. Still, driving in India seems death-defying. Beside the roads, people lived in every sort of shack and hovel, crowded one upon the other. But there were also many luxurious hotels in the cities, forming a strange contrast. The British Colonial tradition is still alive in hotels where the doormen wear huge headdresses and blow long horns to announce their guests, and the lobbies offer welcoming drinks and musicians.

Our tour guide took us to his country village and his brother's home there. We had to walk in, nearly a mile, because the road could not accommodate a tour bus. On the way, we met goats and water buffalo and a camel pulling a farm cart. The houses seemed primitive by American standards. The "bathroom" was a small closet with a hole in the floor, and the kitchen lacked all of the appliances we expect: no stove, no refrigerator. We were told that people still slept on the roof on hot nights. Of course there was no air conditioning, although there were electric lights. Goats and water buffalo roamed the back yard, as did dogs.

We saw two village schools, one public, one private. The students at each were separated onto a boys' side and a girls' side. They sat on the floor, with no desks or chairs. They smiled, and were very friendly. A group of older girls sang a song for us. I remember sari-dressed country women carrying huge bundles on their heads. I remember women at a construction site carrying eight bricks at a time on their heads.

In Jaipur, we saw snake charmers and their snakes entertaining tourists on the streets. We saw carpet factories and showrooms, and I bought a small hand-knotted silk Kashmir carpet for my dining table. I read some of the newspapers, and learned how important our much-maligned outsourced call centers are to the Indian economy. These jobs are very important for developing a middle class. I was left with mixed feelings: are we depriving Americans of jobs or helping people improve their economic situations? For India, the economic impact seems positive.

In Agra, of course, there is the Taj Mahal. This is truly one of the man-made wonders of the world: huge, ornate, and impressive both from afar and from nearby. Since every celebrity, including Princess Diana and Oprah, has had his or her picture taken with the Taj Mahal as a backdrop, I did so too. But I also remember my first view of the structure, from a long way off, from the balcony of our hotel. We saw much, much more in India.

We returned to Delhi for our flight home the day after the tragic earthquake in Pakistan and northern India. I saw the destruction on the news, but since the broadcast was in Hindi, I had to wait for an English-language newspaper to find out what had happened. It's said that some aftershocks were felt in or near Delhi, but we missed those. We flew home the next day without incident.

Looking back at this long essay, I realize that there's something almost surreal about traveling to so many wonderful places with relatively short stays in each. I have learned a lot, but since I'm a rather shy person, I have not interacted with people from these countries enough, even with those who speak English. Ideally, one should live for a longer time in each country and actually share the lives of the people. I think many younger people do that today, and it's a positive trend. If better understanding and world peace are ever to come, they will come through the efforts of the young in all countries of the world—and when extremists stop expecting everyone else to share their religion, whatever it may be, and their lifestyle. We all need to celebrate and respect diversity.

Soon I'm off to Italy again. I've never seen Sicily or the Amalfi Coast, and I'll finally see Pompeii, one of my early fantasy destinations. I still have cities to explore, but I've fulfilled my dream of visiting the seven continents.

On a Country Road in India, 2005

IV. Experiences and Revelations

Jules in 1989

Three Memorable World Events

A few events are so shocking that we will always remember where we were and what we were doing when we heard about them. Three of these events etched themselves in my memory and shattered my complacency, even though they did not physically affect me or my family or anyone I knew.

The first such event during my lifetime was the bombing of Pearl Harbor and President F.D. Roosevelt's address to the nation announcing the United States' entry into World War II. This happened on December 7, 1941, when I was nine years old.

I heard the news in the small room we called the den in our farm home near Whitewater, Wisconsin. The news came through a wooden radio, large enough to stand on the floor and serve as the center of attention in those days before TV. The room also contained a large roll-top desk, a sofa, a chair, and an oblong table with a fringed cloth. The doorway into the living room was covered by a curtain; two dark wooden doors led to a small closet and to the bathroom. Heat came from a radiator situated under the room's single window. The room seemed small and crowded, as was typical in Victorian houses.

As a nine-year-old, I didn't really understand war, but I could tell from my parents' words and expressions that it was a very serious matter. The idea of bombing and sinking ships horrified me. I could almost envision the terror of sailors going down with their ships. None of my family members have ever served in the military, but we experienced war through newspapers and newsreels and the radio. I also experienced the war by buying U.S. Savings Stamps and singing patriotic songs at school, and later, through meat rationing and blackout drills. Our part of southern Wisconsin seemed like an unlikely bombing target to me, but we still pulled the window shades or turned off the lights a few times during air raid drills. I believe that Whitewater even had a volunteer air raid warden.

When I visited the Pearl Harbor Monument many years later, I felt the same horror I'd felt back in our den when I listened to President Roosevelt on the big radio.

The second big, tragic event I remember was the Challenger disaster on January 28, 1986. This tragic event resulted in far fewer deaths than Pearl Harbor, but I felt a more personal attachment to it. Christa McAuliffe, who was to be the first teacher in space, was one of the victims. Even though I was a college teacher, I identified with her desire to learn and to share her experiences with her students.

I was in the microcomputer lab at the old Wright College on Austin Avenue when I heard the news. The lab was a partially-converted kitchen from a previous home economics program, the room that inspired my first published newsletter article entitled, "Yellow Curtains and Kitchen Sinks in the Microcomputer Lab." A few of us believers were struggling to introduce our students to word processing, an innovative idea at the time.

The computers and dot matrix printers my students were learning to use were primitive by today's standards. Still, the computers and the space shuttle alike represented the brave new world of technology to me, and I felt as though someone had struck me in the chest when I heard that the shuttle had exploded.

I saw the explosion and the strange trails of smoke again and again on TV. This was a setback for my rosy view of technology, and the shuttle's having a teacher aboard made the tragedy almost personal.

The third event etched in my memory is the September 11, 2001, terrorist attack on New York's World Trade Center. The horror and the death toll of this attack surpassed those of every previous event.

I heard the news after the first building had fallen and before the second one fell. I was sitting in my condo living room reading a newspaper while two young workmen finished painting the railing of my adjoining balcony. The painters had a small portable radio which they kept at a considerate low volume outside my balcony door. Suddenly, they rushed in. "Turn on the TV!" both shouted. "Something happened!"

The TV news anchors were still speculating about exactly what had happened, but the horror of the incident was inescapable. From that moment, my TV was on during all of my waking hours. I remember preliminary reports of a plane crash in Pennsylvania and speculation about its connection, if any, to the attacks. As the story unfolded, I was spellbound. I guess I'd thought such things could happen only in far-away places, not in the United States.

There have been many other tragic events during my lifetime, too, including tsunamis, earthquakes, floods, and hurricanes. Of course I watched TV reports on many such disasters and contributed what I could to various charities to help the victims. Still, the 1941, 1986, and 2001 events I've described are the ones I remember best. Terrible as they are, tsunamis and earthquakes and floods and hurricanes are caused by forces of nature over which we have little control. War, terrorism, and technological failure are partially or entirely the work of human beings, and to me, that makes them more shocking, and thus more memorable.

In nature there are neither rewards nor punishments—there are consequences.

Robert G. Ingersoll, *Some Reasons Why*

Accuse not Nature, she hath done her part;
Do thou but thine.

John Milton, *Paradise Lost*

Facing Breast Cancer

My early-stage breast cancer was diagnosed in 1990. Although I am still alive sixteen years later, I can never consider myself cured, and it is very difficult for me to read, write, or think about the "Big C."

I'd had "lumpy" breasts, or fibrocystic disease, for many years, so self-checks were difficult and mammography results hard to interpret. However, in spring 1990, I found a small lump that seemed different. My doctor checked and ordered a biopsy.

I was terrified, but we were about to begin our motorcycle trip to the Soviet Union. I insisted on postponing the biopsy. The wonderful trip made me forget, as I had hoped it would.

After we returned, I became involved in creating a memory booklet for my 40th high school class reunion, so I didn't rush back to my doctor. I was feeling fine, and my husband and I enjoyed the reunion. Still, a nagging fear emerged from time to time.

Finally, with my husband nervously pacing in the waiting room, I underwent the biopsy. The news was bad. I remember curling up later on the living room sofa, crying and thinking that my life was over.

My doctor recommended modified radical mastectomy. The choices were one breast or both, restoration or no restoration. I didn't like the choices, but with my supportive husband's help, I decided: bilateral mastectomy and no restoration. I was fifty-eight years old at the time, and at a high point in my career. Somehow, the thought of worrying about cancer occurring in a remaining breast or suffering complications of restoration seemed worse than losing a significant part of my body. I was not concerned about beauty and sexiness at the time, as long as I had my husband's caring support, so that was my decision.

Had I been younger or alone, or had cancer treatment been as advanced as it is today, I might have decided differently.

The operation and the hospital stay were awful, but I've put the details out of my mind. Still, I do remember several details from the aftermath.

My teaching colleagues were very supportive. I missed the first week of the fall semester, and when I was able to return, I looked awful. A few people seemed to think I was on the verge of death, and I probably looked that way. Nevertheless, I persevered. I found out about prostheses, or silicone breasts, and got used to them.

I had to make another decision: radiation, chemotherapy, both, or no treatment beyond frequent checkups and Tamoxifen. The doctors disagreed. I gambled on getting only checkups and Tamoxifen; I was not willing to interrupt my career for treatment. I agonized about this for some time; had I made the right decision?

I gambled, but I seem to have won, at least for sixteen years. I was proud to participate in the Mothers' Day 2005 Y-Me three-mile walk for breast cancer. Yet to this day, cancer still frightens me.

Surviving a Fall

The pain was horrible. It was 6:30 a.m. on October 3, 2001, and I had fallen on the black granite floor of the entryway to my unfinished condo building. I was lying on a floor slippery with drywall dust and other debris that workmen had failed to clean up the day before. As I considered my plight, I decided that my hip was broken, and that my life was over. I'd read many tales of old people breaking hips and ending up in wheelchairs–or worse! As my thoughts grew darker and less rational, I apparently went into shock from the pain.

When I fell, I had just retrieved my *Chicago Tribune* from the small pile carelessly thrown in front of the building and was bringing it in before going to my car to drive to Wright College, where I was to teach two classes as an adjunct English professor. There was no one around; few people lived in the building then, and the construction workers hadn't arrived yet. They were due soon.

After what seemed like hours, but could have been only a few minutes, I more or less came to my senses again, still alone, but sitting in my recliner in my own fifth-floor condo. To this day, I can't explain how I got there. No one saw me, but I must have crawled to the elevator and then to my apartment.

Instead of sensibly calling 911, I called our department secretary, Donna, to tell her I wouldn't be in to teach my classes. I had been Donna's boss for several years until I retired from full-time teaching in 1999, so she knew me well. She sensed the seriousness of my situation and the absence of my usual good sense. I don't know what I said, but I'm sure that I sounded frantic. Donna promised to call an ambulance, and she did.

Within ten minutes, I heard sirens. A fire engine, an ambulance, and a police squad car pulled up to the building. There was a problem–my apartment door was locked. However I'd managed to get there, I had followed my usual instincts and locked the door behind me! I could not get up to open it.

Fortunately, Rob, the construction foreman, had arrived for work by then, and he let my rescuers in. As I was lifted onto a gurney, I asked why the rescue crew included a fireman with an ax, as well as two police officers. I could understand the presence of the ambulance crew, but not the others.

"We thought we might have to break down the door," the fireman said. I think he was referring to both the building's front door and my apartment door, and I imagine that Rob was happy that he'd been there to avoid the destruction. I learned that the policemen were there to file a report, in case I was a crime victim. I assured them that I was not, unless it was a crime of worker negligence.

I soon had my first ride in an ambulance, at least the first one I remember. I'd been injured in a car-bicycle accident when I was ten, but I can't remember how I got to the hospital then. This time I was taken to the nearest hospital, Grant Hospital, now Lincoln Park Hospital, at Lincoln and Webster.

After x-rays in the emergency room, I found out that it wasn't my hip at all; I had broken my pelvis and my sacrum (tail bone). There were no operations possible for my injuries, serious though they were, so I was given pain pills and taken to a hospital room–to my surprise, a room with a wonderful skyline view. I managed to arrange a cat sitter and substitute teachers via telephone. I was soon surrounded by flowers (my niece tends to send huge flower arrangements impressive enough for a funeral). I had a few visitors, but not many. I remember boredom, depression, pain, getting a urinary infection–and to make matters worse, the 9/11 attack on the World Trade Center had happened less than a month earlier, and President Bush declared war that week as I lay in my hospital bed. This was not a happy time.

After a week in that room, I was sent to the Rehab Department: rather dingy, with no view. At first I shared a room with a woman who spoke only German; we couldn't communicate. Soon, I had the room to myself. One of the worst things about rehab was that I couldn't get much sleep. There was a man down the hall somewhere who kept shouting, "I'm dying! Help me. I'm dying!" most of the night. I wasn't allowed to close my door. I wasn't allowed to take down the side bars on my bed. I was miserable. The man wasn't dying, according to the nurse I asked about him, but he must have been even more miserable than I was–or suffering from dementia.

In physical therapy, I learned to use a walker. I watched stroke victims of all ages, one still in his twenties, struggling to learn to walk, talk, and generally cope with life again. I saw people with new artificial limbs learning to use them. In occupational therapy, I had to fold towels and put dishes into a cabinet. I also had to arrange little pegs on a colorful board. I guess I proved that my mind was still all right by putting the round pegs in the round holes and the square pegs in the square holes. I was still in pain; I refused to take enough pain pills to turn me into a sleepy zombie.

I learned about therapy dogs while I was in rehab. My cat sitter, Helen, was a member of a group that brought their trained dogs to rehab centers and senior homes. I saw first-hand how those dogs of all breeds and all sizes could cheer up the patients. Throwing balls for retrieval and giving the dogs simple commands seemed to do wonders for people who hadn't smiled in weeks. It's a great program. I also learned to respect and admire the rehabilitation workers who struggled to work miracles in some very difficult, depressing situations.

After nearly a week in rehab, I insisted on leaving, against the advice of my doctors. I'd had enough. My 69th birthday was approaching, and while I didn't relish spending my birthday alone, I hated more the idea of spending it alone in the hospital. I went home with a walker and a rented wheelchair and what was left of my flowers. This time I got my first ride in a Medivan equipped with a wheelchair lift. When I got home, the entryway floors were spotless, and there were non-slip mats on them–the careless builders apparently had learned a lesson.

Living alone and caring for myself in my painful and barely mobile condition was not easy, but I survived–with fewer negative consequences than I had anticipated. My cat Lyon was happy to see me. My cat sitter continued to come in for a while, and she brought up my mail. I hired the Dust Connection cleaning service, and I ordered food delivered by Seattle Sutton's Healthy Eating. I remember making a distress call to a friend to deliver some toilet paper and other essentials, and two former neighbors came over with all the necessary ingredients to cook me a delicious meatloaf dinner–comfort food, indeed! An old friend I hadn't seen in years offered to drive me to a doctor's appointment.

This experience taught me more about hospitals and rehabilitation and pain than I wanted to know, but I also learned that I have survival skills–and a few good friends who helped me when I really needed them.

My $30,000 Teeth

In January, 2004, one of my New Years resolutions involved coming to terms with my teeth, past, present, and future. I'd had terrible teeth all my life. I had a mouthful of silver-colored fillings (probably full of mercury) and a few crowns of various sorts, but pieces of fillings and pieces of teeth kept coming out whenever I ate a raw carrot or an apple. I saw a dentist about once a year, often on an emergency basis, but that obviously wasn't enough. I dreaded every visit.

I remember with shame my childhood visits to the dentist. I screamed and howled wildly when I was very young, to my mother's dismay. When I was too old to carry on that way, and old enough to go to the dentist's office alone, I found another way to cope. I always stopped at the local five-and-ten-cent store and spent about a dollar on a bag of chocolate candy–a big bag. I ate as much as possible as quickly as possible. In the dentist's office building, I made a point of trying to rinse the candy residue from my mouth, but I don't think I really believed that the dentist wouldn't notice. We both kept silent about the matter. Maybe he was thinking that such bad habits would mean more profitable dental visits in the future. He was probably right. I can't say how much damage all that candy did to my teeth, but it surely was destructive. As usual, I fooled only myself. I've never lost my addiction to chocolate.

What finally got my attention in 2004 was a picture of me taken the previous fall at my nephew's wedding reception. I was smiling, and most of my crooked teeth, especially the one that stuck out at a 45-degree angle, were clearly visible. I had known my teeth were ugly, but not **that** ugly!

At about that time, I'd been watching *Extreme Makeover* on TV. I'd seen lots of ugly teeth transformed. It seemed to take only a short time on TV, and cost was rarely mentioned. I knew it was too good to be true, but I was on a real self-improvement quest. No "drill, fill, and bill" dentist for me! I would find a cosmetic dentist and get my teeth fixed once and for all. Little did I know what I was in for.

When I entered the dentist's office (I'll call him Dr. Smith), my first question was whether I was too old to improve my teeth and my smile. He said, "Of course not!" I proved to be one of his oldest patients, but Dr. Smith was relatively young and very enthusiastic and in search of new patients who looked as though they could afford his services.

The dentist's attractive young staff (nobody with bad teeth ever works at a dentist's office) treated me very well; they soon knew my whole history, dental and otherwise. I learned about modern dentistry. I looked at lots of before-and-after photos. I learned that old-fashioned dentures are out and cosmetic dentistry is in. Any mouth can be transformed, as long as its owner can afford it–and survive the pain and inconvenience. Still full of New Years resolutions, I went for it and signed on the dotted line. I have dental insurance, but it wouldn't pay very much.

I remember that visits to Dr. Smith became a regular routine for several months. I remember pain and local anesthetics and drilling and root canals and grasping the wall as I staggered down the hall to the bathroom. I remember the agony at home later when the anesthetic wore off—I hate pain pills. I remember temporary crowns and permanent crowns and more permanent crowns because the first ones weren't quite right. Dr. Smith admitted that mine was one of his most difficult cases. My teeth had many years to get as crooked as they were.

I ended up with twenty beautiful porcelain teeth, not "Hollywood white," in deference to my age, but a suitable shade that looks quite natural. I also ended up with a bill for almost twenty-seven thousand dollars and an admonition to brush, floss, and see my dentist every two months. What ever happened to "See your dentist twice a year," or my old "emergencies-only" policy? I think the idea of so many frequent dental visits bothered me more than the cost.

I have mixed feelings about this experience. I don't regret it, but I was left wondering how many people could afford such an extravagance, or would go through the agony even if they could. I'm glad that my teeth look better and are healthier, but does appearance really matter? Not much. I'm not expecting any TV, film, or modeling offers. I now dare to smile more often, but is looking better really the key to a happier life? I've been watching too much TV.

This year I went on to get two more crowns for another $3,000 or so. These are necessary, not cosmetic, or so my dentist says. Now I'm optimistic enough to hope that I have had most of the major dental work I'll ever need, both cosmetic and otherwise. I should know better by now.

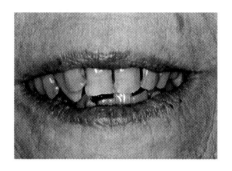

Before

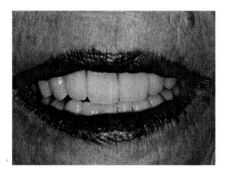

After

Hooked on Sudoku

I have a secret I've never shared before: I am addicted to Sudoku. Sudoku is described in the introduction to *The Original Sudoku* (Workman Publishing, 2005) as "A deceptively simple exercise in logic." "Deceptively" is the key word here. It looks so easy!

Each puzzle consists of eighty-one small squares, arranged in nine columns, nine rows, and nine boxes. Each 3 x 3 square is set off by bold lines. There are always a few numbers scattered throughout the squares: the more numbers given, the simpler the puzzle—or so the puzzle makers say. I don't think so. The idea is to enter the numbers 1 – 9 so that each column, row, and 3x3 square contains all of them. Simple? Well . . .

I first saw these puzzles in an American puzzle magazine. They were called "Number Place" then, and it took me a long time to figure out how to solve them. Once I succeeded, I was elated! I never quite mastered the puzzles labeled "Hard," but I could usually do the "Moderate" and "Easy" ones, as long as I didn't mess them up by putting a wrong number somewhere and getting off the track.

I first saw the name "Sudoku" in *Time* magazine, my source of information on what's new and trendy, sometime in 2005. I realized that this was another name for one of my favorite puzzles. Then my niece gave me *The Original Sudoku* for Christmas in 2005, and I learned the game's history.

Nikoli, described as the "leading puzzle company in Japan," discovered Number Place in the 1970's and introduced it in Japan in 1984. The puzzle can be traced back to Latin Squares (18th century), the older Magic Squares, and LoShu, an ancient Chinese puzzle. The Nikoli editors first called it "Suuji wa dokushin ni kagiru," meaning "It is best for the number to be single." Fortunately, they shortened the name to Sudoku, "su" meaning "number" and "doku" meaning "single."

Suddenly, I began to see Sudoko everywhere: on the

Internet, in the *Chicago Tribune*, in puzzle books in the hands of airplane passengers and McDonald's customers. What was this all about?

Now, I usually begin my day with a Sudoku puzzle or two. I've even been known to keep doing them on and off all day, as I watch the TV news and talk shows and whatever else is on. Talk about wasting time! Fortunately, I haven't had any days like that lately. I still work a crossword puzzle sometimes, but Sudoku is my puzzle of choice.

Why am I addicted to Sudoku? That's a question I keep asking myself. I expected to master the idea of these puzzles and then move on to more productive activities. I think I've mastered the "Easy" or "Gentle" ones, and most of the "Moderate" or "Medium" ones. But note the word "most." Quite often I run into trouble, no matter what the level of the puzzle. Those labeled "Hard," "Extra Hard," or "Diabolical" usually seem impossible, but sometimes I succeed with one of those just after failing at a "Moderate" puzzle.

I'm still trying to figure out Sudoku. All the puzzles look alike. At first I thought that the number of pre-entered numbers determined the level of difficulty. According to the editors of *The Original Sukoku,* no more that thirty of the eighty-one numbers may be pre-entered. In reality, the more common number of pre-entered numbers is between twenty and twenty-four, and according to my unscientific study, there's no consistent relationship between the number of entries and the difficulty of the puzzles.

I have discovered the folly of doing these puzzles in ink; one incorrectly-entered number can throw off the whole process, and it's very difficult to go back. There's probably a principle involved here that I'm unaware of, or perhaps my rate of success is determined by my state of mind at the moment. Anyway, as addictions go, Sudoku seems to be a fairly innocuous one. If my success rate ever approached 100%, I'd probably quit.

Working for Stanley

Once a week or so, I usually get a call from my up-stairs neighbor, Stanley. "I've got three contracts and two letters. When can you do them?" Sometimes it's "I'm out of press kits again," or "I'm going to Florida next month. Can you take care of Gracie?"

My neighbor is "Chicago Legend" Stanley Paul, pi-anist and leader of the Stanley Paul Orchestra and bandleader at Chicago's Pump Room from 1964 to 1972. I think he's the only recipient I know of one of those honorary street dedica-tions: part of Goethe Street near the Ambassador East is Honorary Stanley Paul Way. He also published a book, *Thank My Lucky Stars: a Memoir of a Glamorous Era* in 1999, and his two CD's, "Stanley Paul Plays" and "When Music was Music," provide wonderful music during my long drives to Minnesota to visit my mother. His main business now is playing weddings, parties, and charity galas, and he does it well.

So why is Stanley calling me? It's because I'm his part-time secretary and cat sitter, as in "I'm sorry; my secre-tary got it wrong," and "Did you give Gracie her medicine?" I haven't been a full-time secretary since a short period in 1959 before I began teaching at Wright College, and before that, a year or two at the University of Minnesota Law Li-brary while I was in graduate school. My shorthand is long forgotten, and my typing speed isn't what it used to be. However, I've acquired a computer and word processing skills.

I admire secretaries (the good ones now called ad-ministrative assistants, if they're lucky) for working hard and efficiently at relatively low pay, but I always knew that life as a full-time secretary was not for me.

I talked to Stanley at a condo association meeting just after I'd ended my stint at part-time teaching in 2003 (I'd retired from full-time teaching in 1999), and I was wonder-ing what I would do with all my spare time. Stanley was struggling with a new computer in the hope of doing his own letters and contracts. He no longer needed a full-time secretary or even a regular one-day-a-week secretary, and his occasional secretary was leaving town soon. He was frustrated by his lack of word processing and computer skills. Stanley is a smart guy, but typing up contracts and assembling press kits do not suit his artistic temperament.

I wasn't really looking for a job, and I didn't need money, but I was eager to do something, anything besides reading and watching TV all day. I agreed to help Stanley out. The pay was—and is—modest, but adequate under the circumstances. When Stanley learned that I was a cat lover and cat owner, taking care of his cat Gracie during his absences was added to my tasks.

At first I worked in Stanley's small home office. His penthouse condo is a wonder: shiny black granite floors, a huge, dramatic art deco living room with a grand piano and a fur throw artfully trailing from the back of one of the sofas. Every flat surface, including the piano top, is filled—one might say cluttered—with small silver-framed photos and objets d'art. The retro kitchen is far different from the stainless steel, granite, and hardwood kitchens most of us have in this building. It's large, but compared to the rest of his condo, cozy.

The walls of every room are filled with photographs of Stanley with celebrities: Bette Davis, Judy Garland, Carol Channing, Phyllis Diller, Zsa Zsa Gabor, Oprah—the list goes on and on. There are also many vintage posters and advertisements.

The large outdoor terrace with its skyline view, professional plantings, and huge grill is a perfect place for spring, summer, and fall entertaining. Stanley entertains a lot, both personal gatherings and charity fundraising events. Stanley's apartment has been featured in *Chicago Tribune Magazine* and elsewhere, and it deserved to be. However, if I lived there, I think I'd camp out in the kitchen.

These days, I usually work in my own home office three floors below. The atmosphere and my own computer equipment suit me better. Besides, the constantly-ringing telephone in Stanley's condo is nerve-wracking. If mine rings too seldom, his rings too often.

Caring for Gracie brings its own joys and problems. As I learned long ago, all cats are independent, "senior" cats more so. Gracie is a plump, lazy, sleek, short-haired dark gray cat with an interesting pattern of stripes. She will not allow herself to be picked up. Try to remove her from a chair—or anywhere she wants to be—and she hisses. Try to squirt liquid medicine into her mouth and she squirms away, clamps her teeth, and/or bites. Has she bitten me? Yes, but the blood loss was minor. Gracie *will* lick up her medicine if it's disguised in a spoonful of yogurt.

Let's face it: Gracie is a one-man cat, and when Stanley's away, she's unhappy. She sometimes ignores me completely and curls up under the fur throw in the living room. I've tried to make friends with her, and I think we've reached a stage of mutual tolerance. She's even purred for me once or twice. All cats are interesting, and I can't help liking Gracie for being herself.

Among people in the same general age group (yes, I admit to being a few years older), Stanley Paul and I are as different as two people can be. I guess that's why I enjoy working for him and even look forward to his phone calls.

On Becoming a Fiction Writer

I must be thinking like a writer now. A while back, I found the Winter 2006 *Writer's Weekly* 24-hour Story Contest on the Internet and spent $5 to enter. Saturday, January 28, was contest day (actually, noon Saturday to noon Sunday).

The topic and word limit appeared in my e-mail as promised at noon Saturday. The topic was something about two shabbily-dressed children, brother and sister; an old shopping cart full of cans they were taking to the recycle shack; and a stranger in black who thrust a note into the little boy's hand. The word limit was 1100. From the instructions, I gathered that the topic could be changed or interpreted very loosely, as long as there was some obvious connection.

Never mind that I hadn't even attempted to write fiction since college some fifty years ago, without much success even then. I grabbed a pen and a yellow pad and retreated to my recliner to try. This had to be more fun than watching Saturday afternoon TV. I made up two characters, a mother and son named Mabel and Zach, collecting cans in a gentrifying neighborhood, and I was off. The mysterious stranger became a combination of a thug in black, a mysterious inner voice, and a blond rescuer named Sue.

When I got to the end, I typed up my rough draft on my computer and discovered that the story was nearly 1400 words long. The editing process began. I'd taught English composition and I'd published a few minor academic papers years ago, so I know about editing and revising. I wasn't really happy with my story, which I finally named "An Urban Tale," but I saw it getting better as I removed obviously irrelevant words and sentences.

All of this took many hours and many sheets of paper. I needed to print out each version, return to my recliner, and cross out and write in words as necessary. This went on for some time: to the computer to type in the changes, to word count, to the printer. I tired by 9 p.m. and went to bed.

Early Sunday morning, I read my story again. I changed the title. I changed the ending, which I was never satisfied with. I repeated my recliner-to computer-to word count-to printer-back to recliner routine until I couldn't bear it any longer. The story was 1064 words long, it seemed to make sense, it seemed correctly spelled and punctuated, and I was ready to relax and read the Sunday *Tribune*. I reread the lengthy contest rules, rechecked everything, and pressed "Send."

I soon got a message that my story had been successfully received, and another message just after noon that the contest was over–as well as a notice that the next contest will be on April 29. I expect to be in Italy then, so I guess I'll have to miss the next contest. Will I ever enter again? Probably.

This experience left me with a feeling of elation. Do I expect to win the contest? No, of course not. I don't believe that a person who has never written a good short story can suddenly beat out 499 other entrants. However, I had a feeling of accomplishment! I was a success on my own terms, and it was nearly as good as publishing the Great American Novel or winning the Nobel Prize.

On Monday, I bought four writers' magazines and two reams of printer paper.

My Story: "An Urban Tale"

Dumpster diving takes a lot of patience and skill, and Mabel wasn't sure all the effort was worthwhile. Still, she had to survive. It was hard to sneak through the alleys and construction sites without encountering a squad car or one of those giant surveillance cameras. Mabel had been a teacher, and she once tried to read every dog-eared book she found in the trash, but lately she'd been sinking into depression and despair. As her luck failed to improve, she tried harder to decide what to do about Zach. He should go to school next fall, but it would be hard to enroll him without an address.

Aluminum cans were the best things to collect. Big bags of trash required too much time to sort out, and often contained only scraps of paper and dirty diapers and soggy potato or banana peels, nothing of value. Many cans could fit into the cart, and they could always be sold at the recycling shack. They didn't bring in much money, but a cartful should be enough for a beer and a small burger at the diner on the corner. It was a filthy place, but the prices were cheap.

The beer would be for Mabel, but the burger would be for her son Zach, who trailed her like a shadow on these forays. Zach's father was long gone, and the little boy was very streetwise for his age. He was small enough to hide anywhere. Zach aroused sympathy in the occasional stranger who saw him, though, and he collected a few coins from time to time.

Since Mabel had lost her teaching job for being drunk in the classroom, and subsequently lost their small apartment when the paychecks stopped coming, they'd been homeless. Mabel and Zach went from friend to friend to find a sleeping spot on someone's sofa or floor. It was summer now, so they could sleep in a corner of the park when necessary, but Mabel had to guard her old shopping cart. They had few other possessions.

As dusk fell, the last dumpster finally yielded nearly a full load of cans, but it was late. The recycling shack would be closed before they could get there. They'd have to wait until morning. They could only push the cart under the bushes in the little park and sleep beside it, hoping that no one would steal their cans. Going to sleep hungry was hard for six-year-old Zach, but he'd had the experience before. He was a survivor. With his blond hair and vivid blue eyes and charming manner, inherited from his father, Zach should have a chance in the world, eventually. Mabel? Perhaps it was too late for her. She didn't miss food very much, but being without beer was almost unbearable.

Mabel fell asleep first that night. As Zach lay there thinking about his empty stomach, he opened his eyes and saw a faint light in a house a block or two down the street. It was one of the new houses. Perhaps somebody had already moved in. Zach knew that he was not supposed to go anywhere, but could it hurt to go and take a look? In his tattered blue jeans, gray t-shirt, and worn tennis shoes, he quietly crept away.

When Zach reached the lighted house, he noticed that someone was, indeed, living there. There were no window coverings yet, so he could peer into a low kitchen window and see inside. What he saw there struck him as absolute beauty and luxury. He saw a shiny new refrigerator and gleaming cabinets and counters. Everything was perfectly clean and lovely. Zach hadn't known that kitchens like this existed. In this neighborhood, a kitchen was more likely to be a hotplate in a closet. A lovely blond woman about Mabel's age was sitting alone at the kitchen table. Suddenly, she looked up and saw Zach, who tried to flee. However, the woman opened the side door and rushed out. Zach could probably have outrun her, but he didn't try very hard. He was curious.

"My name is Sue," said the woman. "What's yours?"

"I'm Zach, and I live down there," he said, pointing toward the park.

"Who lives with you? Surely you don't live alone?"

"No," answered Zach. He'd been taught not to speak to strangers, but Sue looked so nice. "I live with my mother. We collect cans."

Sue was newly divorced and childless. She had been slightly afraid to move into this neighborhood, but she believed in economic diversity. She wanted to be a pioneer. Right now, she wanted to help Zach. "Give me your hand. I'll take you to your mother," she said.

Zach was happy to comply; he hadn't had much attention lately as Mabel slid further and further into depression. Hand in hand, they headed toward the park. She thought that they were heading for the shabby dwellings just beyond the park, but Zach stopped at the brush-filled corner. "She's gone," he cried out. "Mommy! Where are you? Mommy?"

"You live here?" asked an astonished Sue.

"No. We were just sleeping here tonight. The cart is gone too. Maybe a robber came along." Zach was crying.

Sue didn't know what to say or do. They walked to the diner on the corner, but Mabel wasn't there. No one had seen her. It would be hard to report a person missing when she had no real home to be missing from.

Sue decided to take Zach home with her, just until morning. For the first time in a long while, he had a peanut butter sandwich to eat, milk to drink, and a real bed to sleep in. He missed Mabel, but she'd been so sad lately. This was much better. He would find his mother in the morning.

As Zach drifted off to sleep, Mabel was slipping toward unconsciousness on a deserted sidewalk several blocks away. Empty beer bottles lay beside her, and she was bleeding from a blow to the head. The shopping cart and the cans were gone. A friendly man in black had promised her beer and offered to help her find Zach, but instead, he'd hit her and stolen her precious cart. Mabel was worried about her son, but now a mysterious and confident voice seemed to echo in her head. "He'll be all right."

V. Adventures and Inspirations

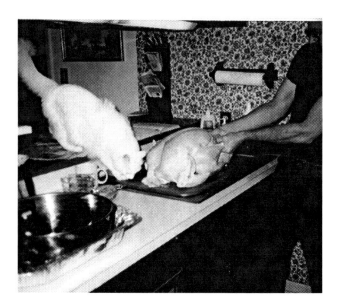

Herbie, a Turkey, and Jules

Susie, a Turkey, and Jules

Anne Hathaway's Cottage

Many of my dreams and aspirations began with Anne Hathaway's Cottage. My first awareness of it came from the framed needlepoint picture that hung in the sitting room in our southeastern Wisconsin farmhouse. I was quite young when I noticed that picture, and since I had no idea who either Anne Hathaway or William Shakespeare was, or where England was, my mother explained, at least as much as a child could understand.

I loved that picture: the thatched roof, the orange chimneys, and the profusion of flowers, pink, purple, blue, yellow, and white, that framed the scene. There were green trees, white clouds, and a blue sky. My practical mother, who was then more comfortable doing farm work than wasting her time on what she called "fancy work," surprised me by telling me that she had worked that pre-printed needlepoint pattern herself while she awaited my birth.

To me, this picture represented romance and beauty and far-away places. At the time, I didn't have any idea where Stratford-upon-Avon was, but it was certainly a place I wanted to visit. That cottage seemed so beautiful, so remote, so much more romantic than our shabby farmhouse. I imagined a world far away, all thatched roofs and colorful flowers, a kind of carefree paradise I could escape to.

Long before I reached high school, I developed a strong determination to leave farm and small-town life behind and become a traveler, a citizen of the world, perhaps a writer—a rich and famous one at that! I was a quiet, introverted child. I lived in my fantasy world.

Then I learned about the legendary Shakespeare and read many of his works. Of course as I plunged into English literature, with its tales of warfare and poverty and other problems, I began to hold a more realistic view of the outside world in general and England in particular. U.S. involvement in World War II began when I was nine, and England started to represent air raid sirens and destruction. However, I never lost my desire to visit Anne Hathaway's Cottage. I was afraid it would be destroyed before I could get there.

In those pre-war, wartime, and post-war days, few people except the wealthy, and later, members of the military services, traveled abroad. My parents had rarely been out of the Midwest, and never out of the United States. I was about twenty-five years old and had just completed my first year of college teaching when I finally visited Anne Hathaway's Cottage. It was as beautiful as I'd dreamed, even more beautiful than the pictures and model cottages I'd collected through the years.

One of the first things I did when I arrived in Stratford was buy a picture postcard of the cottage and mail it to my mother back in Wisconsin. Of course I had a photograph of myself taken near the cottage as well. I still have that photo (see page 63); the original needlepoint picture, slightly faded now, hangs on my bedroom wall.

I've traveled to England several times since and visited Stratford each time. In 1985, I took my mother with me to Cambridge, England, for a summer poetry seminar, and we visited Stratford as well. It was Mother's first and only trip abroad. Of course she admired Anne Hathaway's Cottage too, although she didn't seem to share my passionate attachment to it.

If Mother had similar dreams of her own, she didn't share them. Still, I'm very grateful that she helped to create mine.

The Cats in my Life

Cats have been an important part of my life. When I was a child on the farm, we always had several cats that reproduced prolifically. They were supposed to stay in the barn and live on the mice they caught, with an occasional dish of milk at milking time. The ones who didn't meet tragic deaths under the feet of horses or cows or the wheels of farm machinery often lived long lives.

The first house cat I remember was Purrcilla Mewriel, named from some children's book, I believe, and forever immortalized in a late 1930's show-and-tell black and white photograph. The photograph shows me, a first-grader with long, dark curls and a proud stance, in front of a blackboard on which I'd drawn a picture of Purrcilla, with her name awkwardly printed in the background. Her name is the only thing I remember about Purrcilla.

Then I remember Yellow, named for his color. He was a rather common-looking alley cat, docile enough to let my mischievous young brother carry him around under his arm, even after Yellow got big enough to drag his feet on the ground while being carried. There were other cats as I grew up; I suspect that many of them were eventually victims of the traffic that passed on the neighboring road. Farm cats weren't pampered in those days.

After I went away to college, I didn't have cats for some time. I finished college, earned a master's degree, and then began teaching in West Virginia. There I met Midnight, a shorthaired black cat that belonged to my landladies. As I remember, Midnight commuted between upstairs and my tiny basement apartment, enjoying the affection of all. Of course I had to leave Midnight that summer when I went to Europe, and again when I left West Virginia for good at the end of the next school year. For a few years, I kept in touch with Lulu, one of my landladies, and always asked about Midnight. Then we all grew older, and the correspondence stopped.

During my first marriage, my husband Bob and I adopted another black cat, Cleopatra. She was long-haired and beautiful, but she was a wanderer. We couldn't keep her indoors. She wandered our suburban neighborhood at will, and eventually disappeared. My husband later found her body on Milwaukee Avenue, only a block or two from our house. She was no match for the traffic. Cleo is the first cat I remember really loving–and mourning–as an adult.

While I was still living in Glenview, I began teaching at Wright College in Chicago. One of my fellow teachers, Rita, knew that I'd lost Cleo, and a friend of hers was seeking a new home for his mature Chinchilla Persian cat, Sesame. Sesame was silver-colored and beautiful, with a plume-like tail, and I was in love again! Fortunately, Sesame did not have Cleo's desire to roam, so I owned her for nearly ten years, first in Glenview and then in Old Town. I remember that Sesame was quiet and aloof, but she often slept on my bed. Her hair decorated my furniture no matter how much I brushed her.

For a short time, we also had a young male cat whose name I do not remember. At the time, I thought that only long-haired cats mattered. Then Sesame got pregnant, but she was really too old to reproduce successfully by that time. She had one still-born kitten and another that lived for a short time. I felt sad.

By that time, my marriage was in trouble, and Sesame and I moved to an apartment in Chicago's Old Town. I had my job, my apartment, and Sesame, and not much more. A friend introduced me to an old stray Siamese cat, Charley. Sesame and Charley lived in a state of uneasy tolerance for each other, but Charley eventually died during a declawing operation. I felt guilty, but I hadn't realized that he was too old and infirm for the procedure.

After about three years in that apartment, Sesame and I moved to another not far away. Before long, I remarried, and we bought an old house on Cleveland Avenue, where

Jules and I were to live for more than thirty years. Jules had always owned dogs, and he hadn't even known that he could like cats until he met Sesame; she won his heart. Sesame moved with us, but she was already old and ill. She died, and for some time we did not have a cat. It was best not to while the house was being remodeled, or so we thought.

Eventually, a beautiful long-haired stray appeared at our door. I wasn't eager to adopt a cat at the time, but our friends Keith and Joey convinced me that Susie, as we named her, couldn't survive on her own. We took her in. Susie was plump, and as it later turned out, pregnant when we adopted her. She had an unremarkable gray-striped kitten we named Sylvester, so we had two cats.

Susie turned out to be a wanderer, as Cleopatra had been. The house remodeling was not finished, so we just couldn't keep her in. She became a neighborhood legend. One neighbor emerged from his shower to be scared nearly out of his mind to see Susie sitting in his bathroom. Someone had left a door ajar, and there she was. Another neighbor had a vinyl recliner in his basement apartment, and Susie often walked in to visit and sharpen her claws. She ruined the chair. It was a quiet, easy-going neighborhood, but I think Susie taught our neighbors to be more careful about keeping their doors and windows tightly closed.

I remember that when Susie wanted to come in, she'd hop onto the front outside window sill, and I'd open the window to let her in. She never came to the door. Sometimes she stayed away for days, but just when we'd given up looking for her, she'd suddenly appear in the front window. However, one time she seemed to be gone for good. A few days later, my husband was driving on Clark Street near Lincoln Park when he saw a young boy with Susie in his arms. Jules stopped and said, "Hey, that's my cat. I'll give you a dollar for her." Surprisingly, the boy agreed. I guess a dollar seemed a lot to him then, and his mother probably wouldn't let him keep a cat anyway. Jules brought Susie home.

At about the same time, Susie's son, Sylvester, also disappeared. One day, a neighborhood boy came to the door and asked Jules, "Did you used to have a cat named Sylvester?" Sylvester's body had been found in an alley, and he was wearing his name tag.

Then tragedy struck Susie too. By this time, she was older and rather slow-moving, so a neighbor's large dog grabbed her. She climbed a tree and had to be rescued by ladder. Unfortunately, she'd had a stroke. She became blind, and did not live long after that. I remember paying the mobile veterinarian large sums of money to make house calls, but I knew the cause was hopeless. Susie didn't make it. I vowed that any future cats would stay indoors.

I was ready to give up cats again, but then came Herbie. Herbie was a huge white cat with a big, fluffy plume of a tail, so of course we took him in. His former owners had just had a baby, and they didn't trust Herbie with her. How right they were! Herbie had his friendly moments, but he was rather mean. Once I grabbed him at the wrong time, and he bit me on the arm. My arm became swollen, and I had to seek medical care for a serious infection. Of course Animal Control had to be notified, and Jules joked that Herbie was the only cat we'd had with a police record. Both Herbie and I survived. Herbie embarrassed me each time I took him to the vet. He made so much noise, howling in his carrier, that he had to be given a sedative before the vet could even touch him.

Another thing I remember about Herbie is that he, like Susie before him, showed great interest in the Thanksgiving turkey. I have pictures of both, in different years, poised on the kitchen counter about to pounce on a turkey as Jules prepared it for the oven. Herbie eventually faded away and died of diabetes. He might had lived a little longer if he had been more agreeable to taking his medication.

A few months after Herbie's death, Jules and I got lonely for another cat. We went to the Lake Shore Animal

Foundation, then on Chicago Avenue, where we met Lyon, a mature buff-cream Persian. I remember that he purred when I took him out of his cage. He was long-haired and fluffy-tailed and beautiful, and it was love at first sight.

Lyon was our cat on Cleveland Avenue until Jules died in 2000, and then my cat on Wells Street until he died on December 26, 2005. We went through a lot together. Visitors rarely saw him, but he sat on my lap when I was alone—which was often after Jules died. I learned to give him shots for his diabetes and hired caretakers for him during my travels. His death was a blow, even though it was not unexpected. Even my cleaning woman mourned Lyon, and her job had included cleaning up his ever-present hair and scattered kitty litter. Lyon tolerated her, even when she spoke to him in Polish.

My life with cats has been a roller coaster of joy and sadness; my cats were my children, and they taught me a lot about both love and loss. A cat can be a perfect antidote to loneliness. I suspect that I will eventually find another beautiful long-haired cat with a plume-like tail and fall in love again!

Lyon: 02/03/1992 – 12/26/2005

Media Views on Aging

Is Judi Dench Too Old?

I just read in the *Chicago Tribune* that according to movie exec Harvey Weinstein, "Judi Dench was snubbed by three network talk shows because of her age while she was promoting *Mrs. Henderson Presents.*" Oscar nominee Dench is seventy-one. She didn't appear on *Today* or *Good Morning America* or *The View*, where the stars of new movies usually promote their films. The suggestion was that the viewers wanted to see the young and beautiful stars, not the old ones. Network spokespeople denied any discrimination.

This little story buried in the "Tempo" section caught my attention because I'm past seventy. Don't we count any more? Don't we watch TV and spend money? I know that I do both much more now that I'm older and not working. I go to more movies than I used to. I often watch *Good Morning America* and *The View*. I think I still have all my mental faculties, and I think that Judi Dench is a great actress.

At what age do we stop mattering to the world at large? If the talented and famous are obsolete after seventy, how about us ordinary people? Have the young bothered to wonder at what age they will be willing to curl up and expire? What can we do to fight age discrimination?

By the way, *Good Morning America* included some positive Oscar week trivia today (March 2). In 1989, at age eighty, Jessica Tandy won an Academy Award for Best Actress in *Driving Miss Daisy!*

Senior Lit?

If there are categories like "Chick Lit" for women eighteen to thirty-five, which I just heard referred to on TV, and "Women's Lit," a respectable academic field involving women writers, why isn't there something like "Senior Lit"? I don't think there's much potential for "Romance in the Nursing Home," but perhaps there is. Anyway, there are plenty of educated, mentally healthy people over sixty who have great stories to tell. And many people over sixty are readers who have time to read.

Perhaps seniors have been viewed mainly as sick and poor, struggling along on Social Security and Medicaid, and many such cases exist. But there are also seniors with money to spend. More important, seniors are repositories of a great deal of knowledge and wisdom. They should write and share their experiences before it's too late. "Senior Lit" would be beneficial to both readers and writers.

"With the ancient is wisdom; and in length of days understanding."

The Bible: *Job 12:12*

"Grow old along with me!
The best is yet to be.
The last of life, for which the first was made."

Robert Browning: "Rabbi Ben Ezra"

Winfrey Ticket Scam

According to a short article in the February 21, 2006, *Chicago Tribune*, "Travel agent accused of Winfrey scam," a travel agent in Prince George County, Maryland, was indicted on theft charges. He allegedly stole money from elderly fans of Oprah Winfrey, officials said. The scheme involved charging $500 per person for a bus trip to Chicago and tickets to see a taping of Winfrey's show, tickets that he never delivered. Anyone who has ever checked into the matter knows that getting such tickets is very, very difficult (I've never managed to do so, even though I live in Chicago), but perhaps that information had not reached Maryland.

I guess this is one of the more minor examples of crimes against the elderly, but it's further evidence that everyone, especially the elderly, should check out people and firms they're doing business with. If there's a way to perpetrate a scam, someone will figure out how to do it.

I suspect that the main reason this article caught my attention was that I'd thought I might be the only "elderly" woman who watched Oprah Winfrey's show. There must be others, at least in Maryland.

"One half of the world cannot understand the pleasures of the other."

Jane Austen: *Emma*

Aging is Awesome

In the early morning, I often pick up one of the magazines that accumulate each month beside my recliner and do some reading, with the ultimate goal of finishing the magazines and discarding them before my twice-a-month cleaning woman comes to pile them up on the coffee table, where I tend to forget about them.

Today, I picked up the March 2006 issue of *Prevention*. I guess I read this magazine in the hope of finding a miracle cure for arthritis or a magic weight-loss pill, and on the whole, I find it interesting. I like inspirational stories about women's successes with weight loss, but no magic pill has appeared. I chuckle at the exercise pictures; if I tried some of those contortions, someone would need to call the paramedics to pick me up off the floor. Anyway, today I discovered some inspiring words that seem to fit what I've been thinking and writing about lately.

Geneen Roth, in "Nothing Lasts Forever," wrote, "People who face their own mortality seem to have the same thing in common: an uncommon joy at being alive, here and now, and gratitude for the simple, everyday pleasures that most of us take for granted."

Joan Borysenko, in "I Wish I Knew Then What I Know Now," who has progressed through several successful careers, wrote, "Reinventing yourself is such fun. Don't ever stop doing it," and "Aging is awesome. Particularly considering the alternative." Yes, indeed.

The Bridge Job

According to an article by Lisa Takeuchi Cullen in the February 27 issue of *Time* entitled "Not Quite Ready to Retire," "As life spans lengthen, pensions tighten and workplace rules change, hopping from full-time work to full-time leisure is appearing less realistic and, to some, less desirable." One trend is the "bridge job," a part-time or full-time job typically held for less than ten years following a full-time career.

According to a 2005 working paper from the Boston College Center on Aging and Work, one-half to two-thirds of workers take bridge jobs, and the number of workers sixty-five and over is expected to increase 117% by 2025. While some companies have restrictive retirement rules that don't allow for bridge jobs, others are beginning to realize that older workers have something to offer. In the face of a "brain drain" as more Baby Boomers retire, more companies are expected to revamp their retirement policies. Older workers rate high in company loyalty and productivity, and often prove wrong the assumption that they can't keep pace with changing technology and business pressures.

CVS Pharmacy, Home Depot, and Borders have "snowbird" programs to allow older workers to migrate south in winter and work in stores there. But some potential retirees who would like to have bridge jobs and some companies who would like to keep them are hampered by rules.

I think that bridge jobs are a good idea. I taught part-time for about two years after retiring without its affecting my pension. Even today, I do some secretarial work and word processing, more for fun than for profit. I believe that every retiree with the desire and the ability to take a bridge job should have a chance to work.

"Companies that hang on to their older workers benefit from an intangible, perhaps undervalued commodity: wisdom." We are not necessarily obsolete at sixty-five or seventy or any particular age. Old people matter!

Jack Daniels and the Old Town Pump

On the south side of Division Street between Dearborn and State Streets, there is an advertising sign for Jack Daniels whiskey on the west side of a building. Above a picture of the familiar black-labeled bottle, the sign reads, "Turning Nights into Stories since 1866." I noticed it for the first time on one of my recent longer walks.

I'm not much of a drinker of Jack Daniels or anything else beyond an occasional glass of dry white wine, but this sign caught my attention. I guess it was because "Jack" was once my late husband Jules' favorite alcoholic beverage. He didn't drink much in his later years, but when I met him in 1964, he was a bar owner and bartender who liked to drink some of his own products after work. He couldn't over-do it, though, because his partner was an alcoholic who was seldom sober after noon. Jules held things together.

I met Jules in 1964 when I walked into the Old Town Pump, 1651 North Wells Street, after teaching my evening classes. I was recently divorced from my first husband, Bob. I was thirty-two years old and five or six years into my forty-year career teaching English at Wright College. I was far from my later positions as full professor and department chair, with daytime working hours, but I had a steady job. The Old Town Pump was a popular post-college hangout during one of Old Town's hey-days (the neighborhood has been down and up a few times since). Jules and several employees were friendly bartenders who listened to people's problems and made the diverse customers feel good. The many steins of beer they poured from the taps helped too. So did Jack Daniels.

I lived in the 1300 block of Hudson Avenue then; it was not a great neighborhood, but I stayed there for about three years before moving to a better, safer neighborhood nearer to Wells Street. The Old Town Pump became my after-work and weekend social club, although I was not really the bar-fly type. I met an interesting assortment of people;

many, but not all, of the regular customers were younger than I, in their 20's. Those were the carefree days before fear of AIDS and other STD's. It was interesting to see who went home with whom. I was old enough to know better, but I sometimes drank too much beer and became a participant, though not a major one, in the social scene I had been observing. Mostly, I made friends.

I remember a skinny kid nicknamed "The Rat." He loved to borrow my car, an aqua Dodge Dart convertible with an eight-cylinder engine. Every time he borrowed my car, he got a speeding ticket. No wonder he was called "The Rat." I remember eccentric Bill, who played the bagpipes, walked his cat on a leash, and lived in the same apartment complex I lived in. Bill and I got drunk on cheap beer in his apartment once, but there was no romance. He worked at home as a commercial artist. He used to practice the pipes as he marched up and down on an upper floor of the parking garage. He also played sometimes in the back room at the Old Town Pump, but not everyone appreciated his music. Bagpipes were meant for the outdoors. He played at Jules' memorial gathering, too. Not long after Jules' death, when Bill was in his late seventies, he was one of Chicago's first victims of West Nile encephalitis. His wife, whom he met long after Old Town Pump days, invited me to a memorial gathering at Mike Ditka's on East Chestnut Street. Ditka's is light years away from the Old Town Pump in many ways, but I think Bill would have been pleased.

I remember Don, who had lost his prestigious job as a hide broker and retrained as a librarian. He and Bill and I, and a few others, sometimes rode our bicycles or walked to North Avenue Beach to enjoy the sunshine on nice days. Don died of cancer a few years ago.

The Old Town Pump crowd included several gay men, one of whom became my good friend and occasional escort. He still sends me Christmas cards from his retirement apartment in Palm Springs, California. Jules and I visited him in San Francisco once, and he took us on a wonderful Napa Valley winery tour.

Jules was married, with two children and a home in the suburbs, when I met him in 1964. He also had a passion for some of the customers, mostly young nurses from a local teaching hospital now long gone. His womanizing was notorious. All that made him "off limits," as far as I was concerned, but I eventually fell in love with his charm, liveliness, and social skills. It seemed a foolish and hopeless love.

Since I hung out at the Old Town Pump so much, I became the official photographer for parties and celebrations there: red dress parties, birthday parties, New Years Eve parties. I presented slide shows from time to time, a good way for regular customers to relive the parties while drinking more beer. This unpaid photography job kept me busy, since I never enjoyed a whole evening of drinking and socializing.

Jules divorced his wife in about 1970, after separations and much arguing. I was not responsible for breaking up his marriage; many factors were involved. We married later in 1970. Despite an inauspicious beginning–our friends said it would never last, and my parents disapproved–our marriage was a happy one that lasted until Jules' death in 2000.

I developed a lot of lasting friendships at the Old Town Pump. I occasionally have lunch with three or four women I met there in the 1960's. We're senior citizens now, mostly widowed. We still discuss the "good old days," but many of the old gang have died or retired far from Old Town. Soon no one will remember that the Old Town Pump existed. I still have the official OTP slide collection; I'm sure that bottles of Jack Daniels show up on the back bar in some of those pictures. Yes, as the sign on Division Street says, Jack Daniels–and many other drinks and many people– "turned nights into stories" at the Old Town Pump.

A Tribute to My Husband

His experiences as co-owner of the Old Town Pump throughout most of the 1960's produced many of my husband Julian H. (Jules) Styne's fondest memories. Although he held several other jobs and retired in 1992 after twenty-two years as a Deputy U.S. Marshal, he never forgot the Pump or stopped talking about it.

He and I were both older than the typical Old Town Pump patrons, but since I met Jules there and was a regular observer of the scene, I, too, will always remember. Since Jules can no longer recount his wonderful stories, I will do my best to explain the Old Town Pump as a tribute to the man who was really behind it all, the man I loved and shared my life with for more than thirty years. As Jules often said, "It was not about the drinks; it was about the people."

Approximately ten years after the OTP closed, Jules and I arranged a reunion at Big John's on Armitage Avenue. I believe that this was the fourth biennial reunion, and we had eight before they were replaced by Art Fair parties at home.

In her *Chicago Tribune* "Close Up" column, "Old gang returns to toast 'days that would never end' " on February 22, 1977, Dorothy Collin eloquently summed up both the original experience, as portrayed in a slide show, and the reunion itself.

"The boys wore crew-cuts and Bermuda shorts. The girls wore hair spray and stretch pants.

"They stood with their arms around each other, beer cans in their hands, wide grins on their faces. They looked like they had nothing more important to worry about than putting another quarter in the juke box or a dime in the bowling machine.

"It was the summer of 1965, a typical night in a bar called the Old Town Pump.

"But it was only a slide that brought that long-ago night back. . . ."

Collin goes on to quote several other reunion attendees. A suburban housewife said, "It was such a part of my life for so many years and the people were such a part of my life that I wanted to come back."

Another woman said of the bar that Collin called a sort of continuous, postgraduate fraternity party, "It was like being out of school but still being in school."

Collin described the 1977 reunion crowd this way: "Ten, 12, 15 years is a long time and the faces and bodies that were young then are now approaching middle age. The frat boys look like the Kiwanis Club." At the time, I was 45 and Jules was 48, so we were both good examples of the ravages of time.

By 1977, many of the Pump patrons were doing well. Dorothy Collin's former roommate, Judy Klemsrud, was a writer for the *New York Times*. Marv Kocian was president of a successful "nut, bolt, and screw" company, and lived in Kenilworth. One handsome Irish guy pictured in the slides was in AA, and he didn't attend the reunion. Neither did George Mische, who went on trial with Phillip and Daniel Berrigan as one of the Catonsville Nine for burning draft records in Maryland in a famous anti-Viet Nam War protest. A few former patrons had died, naturally or accidentally.

In a way, Jules was the "star of the show," both in the 1960's and at the 1977 reunion. Collin was amazed at his skill at remembering people he hadn't seen in years. " 'I like parties,' Styne said as he waved at a newcomer pushing through the crowd at the bar. 'You can take the boy out of the saloon, but not the saloon out of the boy.' " That was the Jules Styne I knew and loved.

Jules' obituary appeared in the March 29, 2000, issue of the *Chicago Tribune*. It read in part, "Julian H. Styne, 70, a 22-year veteran of the U.S. Marshals Service who traveled four continents by motorcycle, including a trek through Russia before the fall of the Soviet Union, died Sunday, March 26, of pancreatic cancer in Rush-Presbyterian-St. Luke's Medical Center. . . . He tried out several careers before law enforcement. He owned a live chicken store on the West Side in the 1950's, and in the 1960's he co-owned the Old Town Pump, a lively singles bar on Wells Street. . . . He only discovered motorcycling late in life, but it came to be his one great passion."

Yes, motorcycling was a great passion, and Jules biked almost to the end of his life. But I don't believe that motorcycling ever overshadowed his passion for the Old Town Pump and the friends he made there.

Those Were the Days!

Taking a Walk

I took a long walk recently–about three miles, with a coffee break in the middle. A sunny day with temperatures in the 50's is a rare treat in January in Chicago. Three miles may not seem like much to the young, but for a seventy-something with arthritic knees, it's a challenge. My doctor would be pleased. I took a lot of these walks last spring, summer, and fall, but dreary winter days often make such walks either too challenging or simply miserable. I'm not into suffering.

Yes, I can exercise by using my stationary recumbent exercise bike or a treadmill at the local health club (there's one in my building), but that's quite boring. The bike's in my bedroom, so I do try to use it several times a week. I can watch TV there, but often that's boring too. Why is taking a long walk so much more enjoyable? Sunshine, at least yesterday. It instantly improved my mood. Then, Old Town, Lincoln Park, and the Gold Coast are interesting places to walk.

This time, I headed south on Wells Street. There are shops, restaurants, condo buildings, a Toyota auto dealer, the historic Glunz wine shop, but nothing unusual caught my eye. However, as I traversed the final block to Division Street, I remembered a previous walk when I saw a man, apparently drunk or ill, lying on the sidewalk against a building. I simply walked on. I later wondered why I reacted as I did, with a figurative shrug of the shoulders. I guess that living in the area for over forty years has made me take such things for granted. I walk mainly in upscale areas, but society's problems haven't disappeared. That day I was walking north, and a city ambulance soon passed me, stopping to pick up the man from the sidewalk. The city tries to take care of its problems.

Back to the more recent walk–I turned east on Division Street, crossed LaSalle and Clark and Dearborn, and turned south on State Street, then Rush Street after the two intersected. In the late morning, this area is no longer filled with young revelers as it was when I ventured there at night with my husband many years ago. Are nights on Division and State and Rush Streets still like that? I don't know.

Yesterday, I saw mainly older, well-dressed people, some in business attire, some couples taking a stroll, a few, (mostly younger) in exercise garb. Well-dressed shoppers headed for Michigan Avenue. It's the wrong season for outdoor dining, but in the summer I like to walk past outdoor cafes and observe what people are eating and drinking. In that area, the food usually looks delicious.

I continued my walk on Rush to Pearson and the building site of my likely home in two or three years, The Clare. This is just a construction site at the foundation preparation stage now, but it's to be a lifetime care facility for seniors. I hope to move into apartment 3505, with a balcony and a good view, in about 2008. "An Extraordinary Lifestyle in the Heart of it All," the ads say. With an assisted living facility and a nursing facility in the same building, I hope to be settled for the rest of my life–if I can afford it.

I proceeded south to Chicago Avenue and west to the McDonald's at Chicago and State, where I ordered a small black coffee. It's a great place for people-watching. This is the true melting pot: every age and race and nationality and style of dress is represented. I saw well-dressed businessmen and women, exercise runners and walkers taking breaks, workmen in their hard hats, policemen and women, even a few panhandler types who were gently escorted out by the staff. Anyone who has money to pay is served. There is obviously no dress code. Anyone who does not harass others is welcome. Everyone seems to have a cell phone these days, and I've overheard everything from multi-million-dollar business deals to parole violations being discussed. This is big city diversity in action.

As I enjoyed my coffee, I contemplated my future. When will The Clare be finished? Will it be as great as advertised? Will I live long enough and in good enough health to move there and still enjoy the neighborhood? Nothing is certain, but a woman my age with no children and few living relatives needs a plan.

As I started walking north on State Street toward home, I just enjoyed the sunshine. According to the weather forecast, I won't be able to take a long walk again soon. Rain? Snow? But when the weather's nice again, I will walk south quite often, following the construction of The Clare and understanding why I enjoy living in Chicago.

Lunch with a View

Today I'm having lunch alone at the Signature Room on the 95th floor of the John Hancock Center. I'm seated at a table for two near the window wall on the north side of the building, with a view that goes on and on. It's slightly hazy, but I can see the lake, the ant-sized cars moving along Lake Shore Drive, the Chicago River, Lincoln Park, and probably my own condo building on Wells Street. The latter will take some searching, though–the building is only eight stories tall, so it's hard to identify beyond the high-rises.

I can see the Chicago Historical Society, the Moody Church, Piper's Alley, and to the south, the Dominick's store on Division Street where I often shop. As I look north again, yes, there's my building, with Stanley Paul's penthouse terrace at the top. I can even see my own small, south-facing balcony three floors below. That makes sense: I can see the upper floors of the Hancock Center from my balcony.

Looking back into the Signature Room, I appreciate the pristine white tablecloths and the small purple flowers–real flowers–in small vases on the tables. The recorded music is soothing and unobtrusive. A colorful mural lines the top of the interior walls, depicting waves and swimmers and classic cars and airplanes and nightclub scenes with musicians and dancers. There are other scenes I can't see from my table. This mural seems to create a cheerful atmosphere. It also provides a pleasant preview of summer in Chicago.

This side of the Signature Room is not crowded at this unfashionably early hour. Perhaps there are more diners seated at the larger tables on the south side of the room, where I've eaten several times, but anyway, I prefer to eat undisturbed by crowds of noisy diners. I imagine the room will be more crowded by the time I leave.

The house Chardonnay and the poached salmon salad are delicious! Soon my waiter, Pat, will bring me my white and dark chocolate mousse cake, something I shouldn't eat, but have enjoyed here before, plus a cup of coffee. After all,

126

I need to stay awake through a 2:00 p.m. performance of *Rigoletto* at the opera house.

The Signature Room is one of my favorite places in Chicago. This is my first time alone, but I've dined here with my husband and with friends at various times. One of my favorite memories is Thanksgiving dinner here with my husband some years ago. It was very expensive, or so we thought at the time, but we enjoyed the massive buffet and a small turkey just for the two of us. My husband was delighted to be allowed to take the remains of the turkey home to make turkey sandwiches and turkey soup. Cooking Thanksgiving dinner had been one of his joys in the past, but we'd run out of guests, who had fled to the suburbs to raise families. We had no family. Now that Jules is gone, I often spend Thanksgiving Day at home alone, dining on a frozen turkey dinner, but it's pleasant to remember those earlier dinners, both at home and here.

My eyes and my thoughts turn back to the view. I've never had this vantage point before. Now I can recognize Clark Street and Clybourn Avenue and Lincoln Avenue, all angling toward the northwest. Even in winter, with a dusting of snow and no greenery, Chicago is a beautiful place. Although the sun is partially obscured by clouds, there is enough blue sky visible to add to the beauty of the scene. If I were on the west side of the building, I would be able to see the nearby construction site of The Clare, the senior lifetime care high-rise where I expect to live in two or three years.

To me, the Signature Room is a wonderful place to dine and enjoy Chicago and write in my journal, even when I am, by necessity, alone.

Thoughts on Writing

My List: a Journal Entry

Last night I was depressed again. I'm usually happy and positive on writing workshop nights. What was the problem? I'd been trying to write about my husband's suffering and death from pancreatic cancer six years ago.

What I wrote was really depressing. That story is still too painful to write, and it probably always will be.

This writing experience reminded me of a similar event from January. Every time I tried to find a writing topic, I thought of something negative and depressing. I seemed compelled to write about my faults and my failures rather than my successes, and each effort came to a dead end. What I did was turn to the back of my journal and make a list, and then I was able to go on to find more positive topics.

Here, to counteract any charge of leaning too much toward the positives in my life and ignoring too many of the negatives, is my list. I hope that writing it down and sharing it will bury these faults and failures, or at least my urge to try to relive them.

1. I can't swim.
2. I froze up in piano recitals.
3. I failed physical education in high school.
4. I got a C in speech in college.
5. I failed two important oral exams.
6. I did not earn a Ph.D.
7. I did not date until my late twenties.
8. I had no children.
9. My first marriage failed.
10. I was an inept caregiver in Jules' final days.

Faults and failures should not define one's life.

Creativity

I read an interesting article in the January 16, 2006, issue of *Time* entitled "The Hidden Secrets of the Creative Mind." It is an interview, by Francine Russo, of Washington University psychologist R. Keith Sawyer, author of *Explaining Creativity: the Science of Human Innovation.*

According to Sawyer, creativity involves hard work more than sudden inspiration. Creative breakthroughs require years of hard work, whether in science or the arts. Even Einstein spent years going toward dead ends, and the Wright Brothers kept tinkering with their design for years.

This certainly fits in with current writing theory, so I don't know why this particular article grabbed my interest. Well, perhaps I do know. I have always considered myself uncreative, methodical, and uninspired. I wanted to write great novels and short stories, but I never did. I never even tried.

Maybe my being so uptight about unobtainable perfection led to my depression and discouragement. I had a good, reasonably successful career and marriage, but when these comfortable patterns were shattered by my retirement and my husband's death, I was lost. My clinical depression, diagnosed many years ago, took over, as it has during various times in my life.

Maybe there was creativity behind everything I've done. Now that I no longer need to worry about earning a living, and now that I have nothing but spare time, why not keep trying? It may be too late to become a renowned writer, but I can do some hard work and see what comes of it. According to Sawyer, that's creativity.

Being a Writer

I just decided that I am a writer. No, I didn't get an acceptance letter or sign a contract or complete a major manuscript. I didn't even get a rejection letter. What I got was a different view of what being a writer means. I'd thought of writers as geniuses who got rich and famous by writing best-sellers or wildly popular newspaper columns. To me, all "real" writers were undeniably talented, like E. B. White and Maya Angelou and Mike Royko, all favorites of mine.

One of my childhood dreams was to be a successful writer, but I needed a far more predictable career to earn a living. I didn't have the temperament to be a starving writer inundated with rejection slips. I became an English professor: steady work, but not as much fun as writing. Fortunately, I was in a field that involved writing, but I had a demanding job that left little time to do writing of my own. Yes, some English teachers write, but I just didn't have it in me, or so I thought.

Today, I realize that a writer just writes and keeps writing. I've done a lot of writing, minor though it may have been; I should never have stopped.

Why I Write

I write because it usually improves my mood. There's a feeling of accomplishment in seeing something on paper that suggests I really exist.

I write because I have always believed in the therapeutic value of writing—not just for ex-English teachers and senior citizens, but also for young people struggling to find out who they are and where they've come from.

I write because I read. Once, reading beautifully-written poetry or prose discouraged me because I felt I could never write as well as those authors did. Now, I learn what I can about writing from what I read, but go my own way, as I must, to discover what I *can* do.

I write because I often want to react immediately, to agree or disagree with something I've just read.

I write for myself, not for the public or for money. I'm glad to have the luxury of being able to write what I want, whether or not anyone will ever read it.

I write because I've always wanted to, and because I finally have an abundance of leisure. I write because I find it more enjoyable than watching TV most of the day.

I write because I am a human being who wants to validate her life by expressing it in words.

Chicago Skyline, NW from Navy Pier

Writing for Everyone

Not everyone can be a successful published author. Not everyone is or will take the time to become a master of writing style and grammatical perfection, but anyone with an active mind can write.

One of the best things about writing is that anyone can do it. It's great to attend writing classes and workshops, but you can do without them. It's great to have a computer and a printer and the expertise to use them, but they really are not necessary. It's good to be well-educated, talented, creative, and confident, but few writers begin with all of these advantages. It's great to have a lot of leisure time, but that's a luxury. The writer's basic tools are available to anyone.

The most basic necessities for a writer are a notebook or writing pad and a ballpoint pen. These can be inexpensive and are available to everyone, almost everywhere. Anyone can squeeze a daily five or ten or fifteen minutes out of a busy schedule to write, whether it's in the early morning, late at night, or during a lunch break. It's not a crime to skip a day or two, but sometimes the difficult times are the best for writing. Writing can be a good way to discover and understand the nature of one's problems, large or small.

Writing is a wonderful way to bring what you see and do into sharper focus. When you write about ordinary experiences as simple as taking a walk or eating at a favorite restaurant, you expand that experience by giving it texture and depth that it wouldn't otherwise have. Writing forces us to look attentively at what we see and to interpret it, as well as to remember it.

Some writers keep daily journals for many years. A journal provides a good way to record one's life, not just the major events but changing daily feelings and opinions and reactions to things one has read or seen or experienced. It's a wonderful place to record ideas for future actions and future writing projects. It has the advantage of being private, if you wish to keep it that way. If no one needs to read your journal, you are free from worrying about grammar, spelling, and sentence structure, as well as about offending others. You're writing about yourself, for yourself. Try it.

If you can forget grade pressure and your old English teachers' super-critical comments and exaggerated emphases on spelling, punctuation, or structure, you can stretch your wings. Write for yourself, not for the world or for fame and fortune. Correctness can come through editing and revision if and when you're ready to share your work.

Write because you've always wanted to write, or because you used to enjoy writing, or because you've always thought that you can't or can or should write. Write because you've been told that you have interesting stories to tell, or because you realize that you do. Write because you're bored or sad or happy or disappointed. Write because you have a problem to solve. Write because you're unable or unwilling to do anything else at the moment, or simply because you want to. Write to find out who you really are, regardless of your age or situation.

Remember to observe, think, and write. The results may surprise you!

"If you would be a reader, read; if a writer, write."

Epictetus: *Discourses*

"Beneath the rule of men entirely great,
The pen is mightier than the sword."

Edward Bulwer-Lytton: *Richelieu*

Epilogue

During my tenure as chair of the English Department at Wright College, my colleagues Elizabeth Bouchard, Chris Schneider, and a few others organized the tongue-in-cheek "English Department Committee on Therapeutic Silliness."

For several years, they held annual faculty writing contests: offensive memos, updated proverbs, openings for various types of novels. I usually entered and often ranked second or third.

One year, the contest challenge was, "Write your own Epitaph." I still remember my entry:

An organizer first and last,

She got things done, and did them fast.

As time neared for the final call,

She paused to say, "No rush at all!"

I wrote this epitaph more than ten years ago, but I think it is still appropriate.

Printed in the United States
121450LV00001B/135/A

9 780741 432087